My Twenty Years in Baseball

Ty Cobb

Edited by William R. Cobb

With a New Introduction by Paul Dickson

DOVER PUBLICATIONS, INC.
Mineola, New York

Bibliographical Note

This Dover edition, first published in 2009, is an unabridged, slightly emended republication of the work first published by the *New York Evening Journal* in 1925 and published in book form as *Memoirs of Twenty Years in Baseball*, edited by William R. Cobb, in 2002. A new Introduction to the Dover edition has been written by Paul Dickson and a new selection of photographs has been added.

Library of Congress Cataloging-in-Publication Data

Cobb, Ty, 1886–1961.
 [Memoirs of twenty years in baseball]
 My twenty years in baseball / by Ty Cobb ; edited by William R. Cobb ; with a new introduction by Paul Dickson.
   p. cm.
 "This Dover edition, first published in 2009, is a reprint of the edition published by the New York Evening Journal in 1925 and published in book form as Memoirs of Twenty Years in Baseball by William R. Cobb in 2002. A new Introduction to the Dover edition has been written by Paul Dickson"—T.p. verso.
  ISBN-13: 978-0-486-47183-9
  ISBN-10: 0-486-47183-7
 1. Cobb, Ty, 1886–1961. 2. Baseball players—United States—Biography. I. Cobb, William R. II. Title.
 GV865.C6A3 2009
 796.357092—dc22
 [B]

2008053680

Manufactured in the United States of America
Dover Publications, Inc., 31 East 2nd Street, Mineola, N.Y. 11501

Tribute

The *New York Herald Tribune* wrote on July 18, 1961, the day following Ty Cobb's death:

"The redoubtable Tyrus Raymond Cobb, sharp of mind and spike, is dead. It would take a long parade of superlatives to re-enact his career, for his were talents of unmatched variety. Ted Williams could hit, but his running left room for jeers. Pepper Martin could run, but he was no Babe Ruth at the plate. Babe Ruth became the undisputed Sultan of Swat, but nobody wanted him around as a manager. And many is the athlete who lives the well-rounded baseball life but whose efforts to earn an honest living off the diamond end in the poorhouse. Ty Cobb shone with multilateral brilliance. In baseball (he once held ninety records) and in business afterward (he became a multimillionaire) he scored consistently. After retiring from the game in 1928 his name lived on as a symbol of championship performance. A generation that never came within earshot of his crackling bat argued his prowess and publicized his feats. It is not for us to say that his aggressive preemption of the base paths was or was not in keeping with the book. We'll leave that to the untiring tongues of grandstand umpires. Of Ty Cobb let it be said simply that he was the world's greatest ballplayer."

Contents

Introduction to the Dover Edition

Two names dominate any discussion of baseball in the first half of the 20th century and these are Babe Ruth and Ty Cobb. They are now part of the grand narrative of both baseball history and that of the nation as a whole. Between the two men many books have been written and more are always in the works; assuring that both have survived in the popular mind. But with that both have taken on mythic and sometimes totally exaggerated characteristics. To many Ruth has become a man of total excess and dissipation and Cobb a man of unregulated and unrepentent ferocity. Seldom, if ever, do we hear their side of events they took part in and too often their words are reshaped by ghost writers and collaborators who often add to the exaggeration.

The importance of *My Twenty Years in Baseball* and its rediscovery by William R. Cobb (who is not a direct relation to Ty but an admirer and a fellow Georgian) is that we are reading Cobb in his own voice and as he wished to present himself. Save for the custom of newspaper copy desks grooming the writing for spelling, punctuation and redundencies; one can logically assume that this is the real thing, as real as any oral history. I say this as the editor of a major compilation of baseball quotations in which I reviewed many of the live quotes which Cobb gave during interviews with to the likes of Grantland Rice, Fred Lieb and Ring Lardner which have the same tone, style and vocabulary as the words in *My Twenty Years in Baseball*.

Generally speaking Cobb was an articulate man with an ability to talk frankly and reflectively about himself. Towards the end of his life Cobb granted many interviews which, again, have the same tone. Compare a line which he delivered to actor Joe E. Brown as reported in *Baseball As I Have Known It* by Fred Lieb.

If I had my life to live over again, I would do things a little different. I was aggressive, perhaps too aggressive, maybe I went too far. I always had to be right in any argument I was in, and wanted to be first in everything.[*]

To this one in the book:

My days on the diamond have been rather stormy, due to my high-strung nature and rather fiery temper.

There are many small surprises in this book ranging from his love of fine art and his fascination for another man of strong personality—"I have collected a very fine lot of books on the life of Napoleon. I never tire of reading about him"—to his expose of certain sign-stealing ploys from his playing days. There is also an unflinching account of the hazing he was subjected to as a young player when many of the veterans behaved like thugs. Cobb measures the growing civility of the players in hotels: "There was a time—twenty years ago—when first class hotels would not take ball clubs as guests. Now the most refined hotels in the country seek baseball patronage."

It is also loaded with his own advice on everything from batting stance to base running. In batting stance the feet are the most important element, in baserunning it is the eyes and your ability to see how the defense is reacting. And there is this at the end of a discourse on the art of hitting: "Your job should be to hit the ball on the nose, that's all." Cobb also gives us his all-star teams and tells why certain men were placed on them. As in other things, there is no equivocation in Cobbs' voice: "For third base I have named Jimmy Collins and have stopped right there, I can see no use in mentioning anybody else."

Those looking for the funny anecdotes which are so much part of modern baseball autobiography will be disappointed. Cobb takes baseball as seriously as any player in history and admits that he was never able to see the humorous side of the game.

---

[*] Cobb telephoned Brown a few days later and added, "Joe, I do indeed think I would have done some things different. And if I had, I would have had more friends."

The book is unvarnished, uncensored Cobb and, like him or not, he pulls few punches as he gives his side of the most "sensational incidents" during his playing career. He makes few apologies even for the incident New York in which he was so goaded by a man in the stands that he left the field to beat him. Cobb is forthright: "To this day I believe that under the same circumstances. I would do the same thing again"—and then procedes to give his side of the story.

Paul Dickson

Foreword

These memoirs of Ty Cobb were first published serially in the *New York Evening Journal*, beginning in 1925. They are apparently the result of a significant feud between Ty Cobb and the *Detroit News*, which has only recently been rediscovered.

This discovery came about as a result of Marc Okkonen's diligent research for his 2001 publication, *The Ty Cobb Scrapbook*. Marc's book is a detailed summary of more than 800 baseball games played by Ty Cobb, clearly illustrating the truly exceptional nature of Ty's performance. Anyone who has read Marc's book is struck by the fact that Ty Cobb's performance was truly in a league of its own. Clearly and unavoidably, he was far and above the other baseball players of the day—even those whose individual fame still survives. *The Ty Cobb Scrapbook* is must reading for any fan of Ty Cobb, or for anyone with serious interest in early baseball history. It is also recommended reading for the myriad of contemporary sports journalists who continually repeat the same tired stories about Ty Cobb, while trying to prove he was the bad boy of baseball.

To accomplish his work, Marc Okkonen spent many hours reading and digesting the microfilm of the *Detroit News*, and many other contemporary publications. Here is what he discovered:

On the eve of the twentieth anniversary of Ty Cobb's first game with the Detroit Tigers, the *Detroit News* published a biographical book on the life of the Georgia Peach entitled *Our Ty*. The book, however, did not have Ty's blessing, and that created a major feud between Ty and the *News*. Current speculation is that the book's release was actually prevented, or that it was at least halted before widespread distribution of the book occurred. Despite extensive further research, including a thorough combing of the archives and the library of the *Detroit News*, no further reference to the book *Our Ty* has been found. It is probably safe to assume that, as the absolute premier baseball player in the major leagues at the time, Ty was successful in getting the *News* to withdraw their unauthorized biography from publication. It is also safe to assume that no surviving copy of this book exists.

Certainly, based on his reputation as a shrewd businessman and investor, Ty would have recognized the potential monetary value of his biography. That he later wrote these memoirs himself, and syndicated them for publication with the Christy Walsh Syndicate, is a good indication that Ty did, indeed, cash in on this obvious value of his story—and likely prevented the *News* from doing so.

It seems fittingly coincidental that in the year after the seventy-fifth anniversary of the first publication of these memoirs, they would resurface as a result of a casual reference in a modern work.

William R. Cobb, Editor

Editor's Notes

These memoirs were taken from very poor photocopies of the 36 individual articles which appeared in the *New York Evening Journal* Sports Section between December 1925 and February 1926. Every effort has been made to accurately transcribe Ty Cobb's originally published words. Although the source copy was poor in overall appearance, the actual text was reasonably legible. (See a sample of the original pages reproduced in the Appendix.) Hence, the editor feels confident that this transcription is at least 99 percent accurate and quite possibly even higher.

No effort was made to "modernize" the text. In fact, every effort has been made to preserve the text as Ty actually wrote it. To this end, the Editor has made only the following changes:

Chapter Titles. In the original *Evening Journal* publication, it was evident that the newspaper editors had added the title to each published article. The titles were typically a short sentence that described what the chapter was about. Recognizing that these titles were most likely not Ty's own words, and concluding therefore that they were not a true part of his memoirs, they were not used in this edition. Instead, the editor has selected as a title for each chapter, a phrase from the actual text which seemed to represent a major theme of the chapter.

Subtitles. As was common practice at the time, subtitles appeared throughout the originally published articles. A typical article had two or three subtitles, which were framed in a bordered outline. They each consisted of a phrase of three to six words which hinted at the topic of the following paragraphs. These, too, were felt by the Editor to have been added by the newspaper editors, and not written by Ty himself. Thus, they have been omitted for this edition.

Grammar and Spelling. In the *Evening Journal* articles, there were quite a few errors in grammar, spelling, and in typesetting. The typesetting errors have been corrected. Obviously incorrectly spelled words were corrected, however, in cases where alternate spelling was in common use in 1925, no changes were made. Overall, the editing of words and phrases and the correction of questionable grammar have been minimized to convey the memoirs as actually written by Ty himself. Also, there was quite a bit of inconsistency in wording, particularly in hyphenating and combining words. For example, "baserunner," "base-runner," and "base runner" all appear in the original text, and have been left unchanged.

Photos. The original articles in the Evening Journal contained no photos, other than a single photo of Ty Cobb in the first chapter of the series. The photos in this edition are from the Library of Congress Bain Collection and from Baseball Magazine.

Acknowledgments

The Editor would like to thank many people who have contributed to this work. Steve Steinberg, baseball author and historian, rediscovered these forgotten memoirs on microfilm, and shared printed copies with Marc Okkonen, who was then writing his 2001 book, *The Ty Cobb Scrapbook*. Marc kindly shared these copies of the memoirs with the Editor, and encouraged the publication of the memoirs in book form. Stephen Hoy carefully proofread the first edition of this work, and corrected numerous errors from the first transcription.

The Editor would also like to thank Julie Ridgeway, Curator of the Ty Cobb Museum, and her entire staff, for their diligent efforts to honor the memory of Ty Cobb, and to "set the record straight."

Chapter 1

"Good thoughts grow stronger"

Except for the detailed work of assembling the facts and putting them down on paper I found nothing particularly arduous in preparing these memoirs of twenty years in baseball. I honestly believe that I can remember everything I ever did in my life. To recall facts and incidents comes easy.

The thing that has dawned upon me, however, is how much more important in life it is for a man to remember what he has thought, rather than what he has done. If the average man in any walk of life could store up the ideas that have come to him, few of which are ever carried out, he would be ten times more successful. If he could work out a system by which he could have these ideas or thoughts tucked away, ready to be drawn on when needed, most every problem, new or old, would be simplified. But when good ideas and good resolutions are not executed they are usually forgotten. We remember the things that we did. I suppose that is why the words of great philosophers have lived right down through the ages. Those old fellows kept track of what they thought, rather than what they did. A ball player's good legs may give out, but his good thoughts grow stronger.

Though a ball player must depend on nature to give him an unusual muscular mechanism, the most valuable asset that he can possibly have is memory. He can develop that himself. Unless he does he will be simply a mechanical ball player, passing right out of the picture along with his legs and throwing arm.

This idea impressed itself upon me during the last world's series between the Pirates and the Senators. From the start it was plain to experienced baseball men that the Pirates had a natural superiority in speed and punch. The only question was if they could get themselves in the right frame of mind to use it.

The Senators, more experienced in baseball and in life, started right in using their heads to deadly advantage. Their knowledge and memory completely blocked the naturally superior mechanics of the Pirates.

Next to me sat John McGraw, Honus Wagner and Babe Ruth. We were all there to analyze the games and were determined to do it seriously. Nine times out of ten our ideas expressed in advance of the important play agreed.

I had known of the marvelous memory of McGraw and of Wagner and I soon found that Babe Ruth was much more of a student and serious thinker of the game than the baseball public generally believes. We were all four in the position of what we know as "second guessers." That is, we could calmly await the development of a play and then decide what should have been done. That is a cinch. We enjoyed it immensely. In other great games we had been on the bench, having to decide on the play before it was made. If our first guess was right we won. The second guesser, you see, can always be right. He doesn't have to make up his mind until the play is over. Second guessers are the bane of a ball player's life, and I guess that holds true in any line of endeavor,

It's much easier for the man who doesn't have to think to say what the President of the United States SHOULD HAVE DONE. If he had to tell the President what action he SHOULD take, he would probably be more generous, more thoughtful, anyway. First guessers are the men who make names for themselves.

Having had experience on the players' bench, we older baseball men now sitting in the grandstand tried to be fair and just. I was impressed by the seriousness with which all of us took our jobs. So busy were we with our notes and serious discussions that we didn't even have time for light talk and joking. I find that in airing his opinions in print a man shoulders quite a responsibility. He should not evade it.

The first game had been under way but a few minutes when memories and experience in baseball concentration began to tell. Repeatedly we called the plays before they happened.

For example, Sam Rice was at bat with men on base. Lee Meadows began pitching fast balls to Rice, which past experience had taught us was exactly the thing that Rice wanted. Rice let the first one go, surprised that Meadows had pitched it.

"Gee," exclaimed McGraw, "I guess Sam wishes he had that one back."

The count finally got down to three balls and two strikes.

"If he pitches Sam another fast ball, he'll kill it," we all announced simultaneously. It was such a perfect chorus that we had to laugh.

Sure enough, Meadows did pitch another fast ball and Rice hit it squarely on the nose for a clean hit, driving in runs.

Our memory had been better than that of the young Pirate's.

"Say, Mac," Ruth remarked to McGraw as Pie Traynor came to bat, "isn't that boy a free, loose swinger?" I had turned to ask the same question.

"Yes," said McGraw, "he likes to take a big swing, and he can pick off one outside the plate."

"He'd better keep the ball inside on that fellow," Wagner added.

But the pitcher didn't keep the ball inside and Traynor hit it into the stand for a home run. After that Walter Johnson had Traynor card-indexed. His trained mind won that ball game.

This sort of thing happened time and time again. The Pirates had been fully informed as to the mannerisms of the Washington batters, but they didn't remember. I knew exactly what was troubling them, because I had been through a similar sad experience on that same field sixteen years before.

The Pirates were new at this sort of a grueling test and they were so eager to make a good showing that they lost their mental ease and went "pressing." Luckily for them they got over it much better than I did in 1909, when I went there heralded as a baseball wonder. So much had been written of what I would do and I received so many telegrams of good wishes that I felt that the world depended upon me making a good showing. I thought of every possibility. I went on the field a bundle of high strung nerves. There was much discussion then as to whether Wagner or myself would prove the greater star in the series. The fans didn't figure, however, that I was an overly ambitious youngster while Wagner was a seasoned veteran with an orderly mind that nothing could excite.

Wagner played his natural game. I did not. The harder I tried and the more I felt what I considered a responsibility to my friends and supporters, the more confused I got. My showing in that first world's series was a bitter disappointment to me for years.

Chapter 2

"Pretty well worth while"

Now, as I look back over my twenty years in baseball, the thought has frequently occurred to me: "What have I gained by it? What has it taught me? What have I accomplished? Was it worth the effort?"

In fact, those questions were among the first asked me when I began the preparation of these memoirs. I can see no particular modesty in understating or evading facts that are pretty well known to most every baseball fan in the country. I have won the batting championship on several occasions, and I have acquired my share of fame and money as a professional ballplayer. That, however, would be no answer to the questions that I have asked myself. Certainly, I have accomplished more than that. If baseball success had taught me or gained me no more than that, it surely would not have been worth while.

I could retire from active work right now and be financially independent. I can educate my children in a way that is denied many men in other walks of life. That is a big thing to me. But for baseball, the chances are I wouldn't be in the position to do it. The broadening influence of sound education I regard as one of the greatest things in life. Baseball offers that to young men.

The opportunities offered by travel, observation and contact with men from various sections of the country have broadened my viewpoint on life and have made me more generous toward the ideas and thoughts of others. That I consider one of the greatest benefits of baseball as a profession. One of the first things that impresses a young ballplayer when he comes into the big leagues cities and lives at the first-class hotels is the manners and deportment of the other guests. If he has been denied the chance for education and culture he immediately feels the lack of it and desires it. From that moment on he wants to learn and to understand. Finding himself dealt with and treated as a man of refinement he makes a resolution to live up to that rating.

I have talked to many ballplayers and they agree that their first insight into the broader world and the realization of what education means is one of the biggest thing to be got out of the game. Numbers of them have been so impressed with this as to save up their baseball money and take college courses during the off months. Of course, there are some who do not care and who never improve mentally, but they are exceptional.

There was a time—twenty years ago—when first-class hotels would not take ball clubs as guests. Now the most refined hotels in the country seek the baseball patronage. That is certainly an indication of progress.

My days on the diamond have been rather stormy, due to my high-strung nature and rather fiery temper. Later on I will relate some of these rather sensational incidents and will present my side of them, but not in this chapter.

Through these sensational clashes my twenty years in baseball taught me the necessity of self-restraint. It may be that I have not entirely succeeded, but I have tried. At least I know that a man in any walk of life must learn self-restraint to be successful and to be comfortable in his mind. It requires no effort to get in a fight on the baseball diamond, but it often requires a big struggle and a gritting of teeth to keep out of one. Baseball has taught me that. I suppose the same thing applies to other professions, but in baseball there is much more opportunity for flying off the handle and engaging in physical combat. The lesson is more severe. When men have no fear of each other they soon learn to respect each other's ideas and be more generous minded. They learn forgiveness and manliness. That I think pretty well worth while.

Not so long ago I was seated at the world's series between two men with whom I had quarreled violently. Our baseball quarrels had filled columns in the newspapers at the time. A number of friends gathered around at the series to see how we three would act. These baseball men had been just as fiery and belligerent as I had been, but that day we shook hands and spent a pleasant afternoon discussing the technical points of the game being played. Not a word of the past was brought up. That was because neither of us feared the other, mentally or physically, and we respected each other's knowledge and ability in our profession. That is an example of what I mean by learning self-restraint.

Twenty years of baseball also have taught me the necessity of concentration and application. I have learned the difference between a real idea and one that merely pops up in conversation only to be forgotten. In baseball a player has a chance every day to find out where he is wrong. An idea that doesn't stand this daily test is no idea at all.

When a youngster at the game I used to lie in bed at night and think out new schemes of beating the game—of doing something that nobody else had thought of. That thing of thinking up something absolutely new is a tough proposition. Just the same it is possible to be original if you only stick to it long enough.

Early in my career I noticed that ball players were usually not so fast in the early Spring as they were later on in the Summer. They hadn't worked off their feeling of heaviness. One Spring it occurred to me, therefore, that if I put weights in the soles of my shoes that I would require an extra effort to lift my feet. The work would strengthen my leg muscles early. Then when I took the weights out at the start of the season, I reasoned, my feet would feel light. Without saying anything to anybody I tried out the scheme. When I finally took out the heavy soles my feet were so light that I felt able to run a hundred yards like lightning. I was simply playing a joke on my legs, but it worked.

Another idea that I worked out was the carrying of three bats to the plate so that when two were thrown away the remaining one would feel light. I had seen a batter swing two bats in practice, so I tried three. Baseball offers many opportunities like that for exercising the brain. Most of the inventions in our game have resulted from it. Roger Bresnahan for example, thought up the catcher's shin guards because he got tired of having his legs bruised.

I could name many things that twenty years in baseball have taught me and made the effort worth while.

Travel, study and observation have taught me to love and appreciate fine paintings. I have been able to see things that otherwise I might never have known about. I am fond of reading history, for instance. I always like to read about places that I have seen. I have collected a very fine lot of books on the life of Napoleon. I never tire of reading about him.

I also have learned to love and appreciate music.

I am not alone in this. These educational benefits have come to scores of ballplayers.

Yes, after all. I think it pretty well worth while.

Chapter 3

"Beginning to feel the difference"

I don't want this autobiography to be considered my valedictory. I am not through as a ballplayer. Frankly, though, I realize that I am not as good as I was. It is my present intention to take part in a little more than half the games next year (1926), but not all.

While I sat in the press box at the last world's series and dictated my opinions of the play, someone asked me if I believed that I could hit the ball as well as ever.

"Certainly not," I replied. "I am beginning to feel the difference."

This remark appeared to surprise my companion.

"You are the first ball player I ever saw," he remarked, laughing, "who would admit that he was not as good as he used to be, especially with the bat."

That, I think, was an exaggeration. I know several players who realize that they are on the decline. How could a man of common sense think otherwise?

On that very day Walter Johnson was winning the opening game for the Senators. Nobody knew better than Walter Johnson that he was not the great Walter of days gone by, but by cleverness and skill he was able to make those younger Pirates think so.

The first symptom of a ball player having passed the zenith is felt in the legs. Even a pitcher's legs weaken before his arm

does. Good legs are just as important to a pitcher as to an outfielder. He gets his pivot from the legs. An experienced manager on the bench can note these symptoms almost as quickly as
the player himself.

Johnson knew quite well that the Pirates would attack him in
his weak spot and would attempt a bunting game as soon as the
opportunity offered. To offset this he aimed his whole effort at
keeping the ball out of bunting range. Rarely did he pitch a low
ball when there was a runner on base. It is almost impossible,
you know, for a batter to bunt a ball that crosses the plate above
his waist. By marvelous skill and a close study of the individual
batters this old master outwitted his younger and faster opponents for two games. Finally, they attacked him in his vital
spot.

A year before, when the Giants lost the final game against
Johnson, I was amazed—I might say, delighted—to note, that as
wily a manager as John McGraw did not get an attack organized
at Johnson's legs, rather than his arms. If you will remember
that far back, George Kelly struck out trying to score Frank
Frisch from third when a bunt might have turned the trick.
That, though, is second guessing of the worst form, and I won't
be guilty of it again.

I mention this merely to emphasize my point that the legs of
a ball player go first. It is the lack of springiness in taking that
first jump for a fly ball, or in starting for first on an infield hit,
that tells a man how much he is slipping. That is why I know I
am not as good as I used to be. The old spring in the legs that
sent me forward first is partly missing.

As to the eye, it is practically always the same. The eye, however, cannot do all the hitting. The legs have got to finish what
is started by the eye. To fool an old batter like Hans Wagner, or
even Wilbert Robinson, would be difficult to this day. John
McGraw tells me that he can still gauge the ball as well as ever.
The eye informs the experienced batter correctly, but the muscles, having lost that zippy spring and the natural coordination,
cannot make use of the information.

So, in my opinion, the ball player who, after nineteen years on the diamond, declares that he is just as good as ever, is not only kidding his listeners, but is committing the greatest mental crime of all—kidding himself.

The success of most great men has been due to a full understanding of their weakness or strength and a willingness to admit it frankly—at least to themselves. Failures are largely due to men kidding themselves.

That willingness and ability to understand one's self has a double advantage. The man who is wise to his own ability is usually wise to that of his opponents. It is pretty hard to hide a weakness from an opponent who knows his own weakness as well as his strength.

I have made many a successful play by testing the other fellow's nerve before he had a chance to test mine. There is always a great advantage in creating the problem for the other fellow to solve, rather than permitting him to put you to the test. I guess that is just another way of expressing what is called aggressiveness in baseball. The principle is just the same in any walk of life. The timid undetermined man is always put to the job of guessing nearly all his life. The aggressor makes him do it.

Baseball players, like men in most any walk of life, I suppose, are divided into two classes. These two classes are described by some wise old manager, who said: "The topnotchers are those who try to find their faults and correct them. The failures are those who try to hide, or cover up, theirs."

The constant use of the alibi has spoiled many a great baseball career. The fellow, who comes back to the bench after a bad play and says: "Why I thought so and so," usually didn't do anything of the kind. If he had thought he wouldn't have done it.

When I was twelve years old I knew pretty well what I could do as a ball player. This was not cocksureness nor conceit. In fact, I was rather timid as a small boy especially in the presence of my elders. I didn't lack in aggressiveness, however. Just the same, I had that gift of being able to appraise myself, even at that age. It has been my greatest asset in life.

It might surprise you to know that I played on a team with the grown-up boys at the age of twelve. The intense respect instilled in me for these older boys, and, their kindly consideration for my youth, developed in me the characteristics that got me into so much early trouble in the big league—that mystified me so at the attitude at my team mates. But that is a story I will take up later.

Chapter 4

"I took to baseball naturally"

That this chronicle may start correctly, and that there may be no mistake about my age, I was born at Narrows, Georgia, on my grandfather's plantation, December 18, 1886 and was christened Tyrus Raymond Cobb.

This, as you know, is near Royston, Georgia, a small country town of the old type. It was there that I learned to play baseball; rather, that I got fascinated. I was always active physically and fast on my feet. I took to baseball naturally.

The atmosphere of the community in which I was brought up offered as little encouragement, perhaps, as any place in the world to a boy who had ambitions to become a professional ball player. We had a team at Royston, a good one, too, and we had exciting games between neighborhood teams, but the thought of professionalism had never entered our heads. My father was William Herschel Cobb, a school teacher at Royston. He was also County School Commissioner and later was elected to the State Senate, where he did some great constructive work on the public schools of our State.

It is needless for me to say that my father was very strong in his opposition to baseball, particularly as a profession. In fact, such a thing as that had never occurred to him.

It has struck me as odd that of all the baseball autobiographies I have read not one of the successful players ever started out with the full consent of his father. Parents are unanimously

13

against baseball as a profession. Many of them think it degrading—or used to be—while others look on it as a mere waste of time, just when a young fellow should be planning his future career and position in life. I think it mostly apprehension. These parents can not be expected to understand that baseball is an honorable profession and that a boy may succeed in that as well as in any other calling. I would even hesitate right now to encourage my own son to enter a baseball career. Most all ball players feel the same way.

I was discussing this with a newspaper man the other day.

"Would you want your son to become a newspaper man?" I asked him.

"No, indeed," he said. "It's a hard way to earn a living—too uncertain."

Now, I know my friend would be tickled to death to have a son a great newspaper man. Parents hate to see their sons go through the hardships that they have suffered.

That same feeling applies to baseball.

The most ardent admirer any good ball player ever had was his father—the very same father who objected so strenuously to his starting. Go to any World's Series and you will nearly always see the fathers rooting for their boys, and they will leave nobody in doubt as to whose fathers they are.

Pronounced success in many walks of life very quickly wipes out all parental objection to that particular profession.

A successful ball player can do a great deal of good. He does as much as any other public character to give people recreation and to keep in them the thrills of youth. His is, in a way, a position of trust. The lowest form of man is one who would betray that trust. Evidence of this is the widespread revulsion over the few cases of baseball dishonesty. If people did not take their baseball to heart such incidents would not even attract casual attention.

The man who tells you that baseball, as a national game, is crooked does not really believe anything of the kind. If he did he would not be concerned about it.

My father's plans for me contemplated graduation from Annapolis or West Point. When I was old enough he did get me an appointment to Annapolis. I couldn't quite satisfy my mind with going to a naval school for four years. Somehow it had no fascination for me. I was eager to be doing something. I had the same feelings toward being shut up in the Military Academy at West Point for four years or more. I had the feeling, of course, that I must have a college education, but I wanted to be active and with a bit of freedom in summer while taking my course. We didn't know so much about athletics at the naval and military academies then.

Naturally my mind centered on the University of Georgia. Mind you, these problems were all discussed and considered when I was little more than twelve years old. And being a pretty good kid ball player I had ambitions to be a great player on the college team when I was old enough. I had never thought of professional baseball.

During my twelfth year I received what I regarded a great honor in being put on the first nine at Royston with the grown-up boys. They needed a shortstop and thought I could fill the bill on account of my hitting and speed.

If I do say it myself I filled the bill acceptably. We wore bright red suits, and, believe me, whenever the Royston club went on the field they attracted attention. You could see that club a mile.

We used to play games at Anderson, S.C., and Hartwell, Georgia. Pretty soon I had a little reputation as a kid ball player that made me mighty proud and ambitious. I began to ask questions and to sense possibilities in baseball. My ambition was to show up at the University of Georgia and be regarded as a real ball player in my freshman year.

I don't recall whether it was by accident or study that I developed a snap swing at the ball that made me a good hitter, even at that age. The pitchers never fooled me much. I learned that the way to hit a ball sharply was to meet it in front of the plate just as it broke. That is how I developed the habit of holding the bat with my hands apart, well up on the handle. I have always batted that way. Hans Wagner batted the same way. He tells me that style came to him just as it did to me.

Two or three years ago one of the bat manufacturers got out

a little book on how to bat. Pictures were given of all the different styles. It was pointed out that Cobb and Wagner both used the style of keeping their hands apart on the bat handle. A note said, however, that this style wasn't recommended. Wagner and I both had a laugh about that. At the time we were both leading our leagues—in a style not recommended.

While I was with Royston the incident occurred that suddenly turned my thoughts to professional ball.

Chapter 5

"Satisfying my ambition"

It was a trivial thing that overthrew all the plans of myself and of my father for my college career. I suppose that the lives of most men are thrown into an entirely new channel by some such unexpected incident.

A player on our Royston Reds, Van Bagwell, went up to Nashville on a trip and saw some Southern League baseball. There they had heard of him. Scouts were not as numerous then as now and much of the search for new players was done by letter. Inquiries of this kind had been made about Bagwell.

While in Nashville he was given a trial by Newt Fisher, then manager of the Nashville team and one of the best known of the old-time baseball men who were prominent in the minor leagues.

I was sixteen years old by this time and my four years with the Royston Reds had built me up into a big, strong fellow. I hope I am not immodest in saying that I was then quite a ball player for a boy who had never had any experience except in a little town. I had the fundamentals. I could hit, run and field. Once a boy can do those things naturally all he needs is the training in the finer points of the game. I was eager to learn more.

For days and days we talked about Van Bagwell being up there among the minor leaguers—a professional and making good. It fired us all with ambition and wonder.

Finally we got a letter from Van Bagwell telling all about the

professional league, how the players acted, what was expected
of them, and so on. He told about the life in the hotels. Every
line of his letter was fascinating. I read it and reread it. I didn't
realize it for a long time, but my future had been mapped out
for me. Nothing could keep me from satisfying my ambition of
showing that I could be as good as any of them.

I was still too modest to think of the Southern League. There
was a professional team at Augusta, my present home, which
was nearer. Augusta was in a league a grade lower than the
Southern, the Southern Atlantic League.

The Van Bagwell letter having given us all a new line of
thought. A friend of mine wrote to Con Strouthers, manager of
the Augusta team, about me. Later Con Strouthers wrote to me,
wanting me to come to Augusta and talk to him—at my own
expense.

I go into all this detail for the purpose of showing just how the
average professional ball player gets his start. All of them go
through the same thing, or nearly so.

The letter from Strouthers was a bombshell in our home. To
say that I was excited would be putting it mildly. I was fairly
consumed with a desire to display my ability on a league diamond with professional ball players. My father was shocked.

Never in my life had I had an argument with my father. Boys
in my section of the country accepted family discipline as a matter of course. We were supposed to respect our father's wishes
without whining or quibbling. I knew that the biggest moment
of my life faced me. I would have to face my dear father, man
to man, and have it out. My mind was made up. I knew that
nothing would turn me. At the same time I did not want to
oppose him.

My father called me into his study. Beginning in a calm voice
he tried to dissuade me by pointing out the loss I was bound to
sustain by giving up the career that had been planned for me.
He didn't understand anything about professional baseball, but
could see no future in such an undertaking for his son. His arguments were sound and logical. I knew that. Just the same, I
wanted to satisfy my ambition. I was eager to enter into compe-

tition. We discussed it for fully an hour, the son getting more obdurate all the time.

"All right, son," he finally said, a note of sadness in his voice, "as long as you are so determined I will consent for you to go. I want you to go right, though, and be a gentleman."

From a drawer he drew a check book and proceeded to write out a check. I hadn't expected that. The check was for fifty dollars.

"If you are embarrassed let me know and I will send you more, and, as long as you are determined on this experiment, I want you to win. You must keep in touch with me."

My father was not a rich man and, realizing what this meant to him, a lump came up in any throat. I had never realized up to that point just how wonderful a man my father was. I have an idea that he thought I would get through with this adventure and come home ready to start life on a sound basis.

Stewart Brown, now a famous surgeon, went with me to Augusta. We both carried our Royston uniforms of that brilliant red.

My meeting with Strouthers impressed me. He gave me a trial and agreed to sign me for $90 a month. I presented to him a letter of recommendation from our preacher as to my character and bringing up. I didn't understand then why Strouthers smiled.

"But you'll have to get rid of that red uniform," he told me. "We'll get one of the regular uniforms for you."

Ordinarily there wouldn't have been much chance for me to get in a game, but Harry Bussey, a veteran, had been declared ineligible for having played with an outlaw league.

"He won't be allowed to open up with Augusta," Strouthers told me, "so I'll let you play centerfield until things are straightened out."

I played two games. I'll never forget my first trip to the plate in that big league uniform. Fans hardly realize what a thrill that is to a young ball player. I did not have stage fright. In fact, I got hold of a curve and hit it squarely on the nose for a home run. Later in the game I got a two-bagger.

Now I felt myself made. I had heard that first applause from a league crowd.

The next game I did well again. I was in the clouds. And then Harry Bussey was reinstated. Con Strouthers sent for me. I was released.

Chapter 6

"Don't come home a failure"

After having hit a home run and a two-bagger in my first two games in a league, the sudden notice that I had been released came as a bitter disappointment.

To this day I think Con Strouthers might have kept me a little longer. Evidently he didn't understand a boy's mind. But Harry Bussey, being a veteran and having been reinstated, was entitled to a job. They couldn't afford many substitutes in those days and on that kind of a team.

Even in my despair I felt it my duty to call up my father.

"Father," I told him over the telephone, "I have been released."

"Is that so?" he replied, and I can hear his voice right now.

"It was not on account of bad playing," I said, and explained the circumstances.

"But," I went right on, "I have been offered a job in the Tennessee-Alabama League."

That league was a notch lower in classification than the South Atlantic League.

"Well, son," said my father over the phone, "that is unfortunate—being released after two days—but, my boy," he added in tone that electrified me, "don't come home a failure."

This sympathy and encouragement, this way of instilling in me the principle of fighting a battle until it is won helped me more than any lesson I have had in my life. I saw my father, a dignified

professor, in a new light. I loved, admired and respected him
more than I ever had before. For his sake, now, I was determined to win if I had to give up a leg or an arm in doing so.

I accepted the offer from the little Tennessee-Alabama
league and went to join the Anniston team. There I played my
head off, as we say in baseball. I concentrated every thought on
mastering my new profession. I made good, too.

Dad Groves was the manager of the Anniston club and he
gave me every help and encouragement possible. He seemed to
understand better. In fact, a life of hard knocks and experience
had given him a broad understanding of human nature in general. He handled his players as individuals. They all loved him.

And, it so happened, toward the end of the 1904 season—my
first year in professional baseball—that Andy Roth succeeded
Con Strouthers as manager of Augusta in the South Atlantic
League. I had refused to go back to Augusta to play for
Strouthers, but when Roth sent for me I came flying.

Here I am back near home with the satisfaction of having
played out a season of league ball and ready to start in higher
grade.

That club managed by Andy Roth developed a great spirit.
Every man on the team was proud of it, and all of us worked
together like a machine.

Roth started the 1905 season with good players and as the
season went on they got better. I don't remember ever having
known of a minor league club that had as many players who
afterward gained big league reputations. All of this I attribute to
Roth's wonderful insight into a boy's nature, even if he didn't
make us succeed collectively.

On that Augusta club, where I really began to attract attention higher up, were Andy Roth, Clyde Engel, Pucky Holmes,
Nap Rucker, Eddie Cicotte, Polchow, Browne, George Leidy
and myself.

With Augusta I got off to a good start and, profiting by what
I had learned the first year, I soon had a reputation as a good
batter and a base runner. Being a native son the fans encouraged me at all times.

Naturally news of the individual success of young Cobb got

back to Royston, but a short distance away. The people were just as proud of Nap Rucker and could say nothing but good things about our team mates who were not of the soil as we were.

My father had become editor of the local paper, in addition to his other duties. So much had been said of his son that, to my delight, he was converted. He suddenly became a baseball fan.

And when a father who had objected to professional baseball learns to enjoy the sport of it he becomes the most rampant of fans. Mine was no exception.

So great had become the baseball enthusiasm in Royston that my father decided to write up the local games in the paper—the Royston games, I mean. There was no reason he figured, why Royston shouldn't have a baseball column as well as the big papers.

So, taking pen in hand, my father wrote up the account of a game played by the Royston Reds. Believe me, he bore down on the adjectives. That he was a thorough convert and an enthusiast was clearly proven in that remarkable story. With plenty of space and time he let himself go.

The whole town was surprised for he was so dignified.

Now, the tide had turned; instead of father having converted me to Annapolis or West Point, I had converted him—at least the game had—to a baseball fan. I was indeed happy.

A little way back I spoke of George Leidy. He was a veteran who understood baseball and baseball people thoroughly, having been in the game all of his life. He later became my manager, succeeding Roth. From him I learned much. He was never too busy to go into details and explain things to me. Through him I began to see the hundreds of things one must learn in the game; the correct move in tight situations.

Leidy was a picturesque character who talked with a drawl and always had something funny to tell. Back of it all, though, there was a head full of sound, common sense. He taught me the many variations of the hit and run play, the trick of hitting behind the runners, and Leidy was one of the biggest forces that made me a success. I want to talk more about him later.

Chapter 7

"A foolish thing to do"

To my mind the most unwise trait a man can have is to take his profession or business lightly. No matter what a young fellow's calling may be, if he doesn't consider it seriously and thoughtfully, the chances are a hundred to one that he will be either a partial success or a complete failure.

That principle holds good in any kind of endeavor. It is almost immediately noticeable in baseball. There have been many great wits and clowns in baseball—men with rare natural ability—but not one of them has ever been an outstanding star. This was entirely due, I think, to their inability to take their work seriously.

I had my lesson right at the start and it was a valuable one. I have never been so evenly balanced that I could concentrate on my work one minute and see the funny side of it the next. I don't know if I am lacking in a sense of humor, but I have never been able to see the comical side of baseball until it was pointed out to me by somebody else.

I know what it is, though, to take a ball season as a joy ride and look upon it as a Summer's vacation. That is the trap I fell into a few months after I had earned myself a regular place on the Augusta team in the South Atlantic League.

On our club we had some great individual players, men who afterward became famous, but collectively they went about the country at first like a picnic party.

George Leidy, the old minor league manager, brought us out of that after he had succeeded Andy Roth as manager.

24

We were playing Savannah. None of us had been taking things seriously. I was eighteen years old, with all the spirit and tendencies of a boy of the age. I was making what was then considered a good salary and baseball began to look to me like one of the greatest larks in the world.

This day in Savannah we had stopped the popcorn boy and several of us sat on the bench munching at those big cakes of popcorn crackerjack. I went out to centerfield carrying the popcorn in my hand. I know now how bad it must have looked, but nobody said anything to me at the time.

I was standing in my position, munching away and making light remarks to the other players, when a high fly ball was hit directly toward me. I don't know what possessed me that day, but I didn't want to drop that popcorn. Neither did I want to miss that fly ball. I was afraid if I didn't throw the popcorn away I might miss the ball and I also felt that if I caught the ball I would lose my popcorn. In a feeling of boyish bravado I then tried to see if couldn't hold on to the crackerjack and still catch the ball.

Well, you can easily imagine what happened. I lost both.

The missing of that fly ball had some effect on the game, too.

When I came back to the bench I knew that Leidy's eye was boring into me.

"That was a foolish thing to do," he said to me in that high-pitched drawl. "Don't ever do that again."

Later he took me off privately and gave me a lecture that would be valuable to any boy in any walk of life.

"Son," he said, "if you expect to get anywhere you have got to take your business seriously. The game of baseball is too big a thing to be considered that way. If all the players went at it in that spirit the game would become a joke and would die out in a few years.

"Did you ever stop to think," he went on, "what baseball does for many a young man who would never have any chance otherwise to make a good living and travel about the country? You have had the advantage of early education, but most of the players have not. By studying their profession and making a success of it they can get an education that way. Besides, it isn't fair to your employer or to yourself to make a hippodrome out of baseball. I don't care what kind of skylarking you do outside. But when you get on that ball field I want you to work at it and study every angle with just as much seriousness as if the welfare of the country depended upon it. You've got a lot to learn and you've got great possibilities. I know you don't want to be a failure."

Every word of this from the kindly old fellow burned into me. I knew he was right. I admitted the truth of his words and promised him that I would never do such a thing again. And I certainly have kept that promise. His words cured me. Many young fellows have been failures, simply because they did not have a George Leidy to straighten them out.

After I got into the big league I heard Hughie Jennings say one day that the success of himself and John McGraw and Willie Keeler was due entirely to the mental concentration and physical work they put into the study of their business.

They used to go out and work for hours to correct some mistake they had made the day before. They did it in hours that the rest of the club was resting. Any job that is worth doing is worth doing right, and they were quick to see that.

The profession of baseball offers to many young fellows an opportunity that they could never have in any other line. In the first place, no education is required. By becoming proficient they can earn just as big salaries as men who save spent years going through college. They are enabled to get about the country and study the ways of people. They become broadened and in these pick up by observation the education that was neglected in their youth. It is a thing well worth striving for.

Men like Leidy and others appreciated that more than I did at the start. That kindly talk, however, gave me the viewpoint. A baseball career really is too serious a thing to permit of trifling.

Right then and there I made up my mind to concentrate my whole thought on the game and, if possible, to make of myself as big a star as my natural ability would permit. That is why, I believe, I have never been able to enjoy the humorous side of the game as much as others.

Chapter 8

"Regulate the food"

Amost vital factor in baseball and one most frequently disregarded is diet. The popcorn incident, mentioned in my last article, which brought home to me the seriousness of my new profession, also served to help me in the matter of understanding my physical condition.

This thing of knowing when and how to eat is just as applicable to the banker, the lawyer, the broker, the merchant, the writer and the actor as to the ball players. The difficult thing is to impress it upon the mind of the young fellows who are blessed—or cursed, according to how old you are—with that constant appetite. I have come to the conclusion that no male person ever really knows how a boy should act until he has one of his own.

For example, how much better care would you take of your teeth if you had to start all over again?

After George Leidy had pointed out to me what a reflection it was on my profession to be eating popcorn while playing the outfield, he suddenly remarked:

"And it's a bad thing for your stomach. You can't be active physically while your digestion is working."

That thought came home to me a few days later. In the hotels where all kinds of food was set before us to be eaten at the expense of the club we used to pitch right in and enjoy it to the last dish.

One day at lunch we had a dish of roast pork and sweet potatoes, my favorite, and I let nothing stand in my way. That afternoon, in the game, an odd feeling of heaviness came over me, something that I never had experienced before. I couldn't get the spring in my legs and even in swinging the bat I seemed to lack snap. I couldn't get that important first jump in going for a fly ball.

"What's the matter with you, boy?" Leidy asked, worried.

"I guess it's the big lunch," I told him.

"Now," he told me, "you've got to remember that smart ball players are the ones who take care of themselves. There's no use in us trying to control a player's eating. Unless he sees the necessity of it himself he'll never learn. I am sure you are not that kind of a boy."

I did see the necessity of looking after the diet right away.

"Either get up early and eat a light breakfast and then a very light lunch," Leidy advised me, "or get up late and eat a good breakfast, so as to skip lunch all together. Too much food in the stomach will make you sick when you are taking exercise."

When a boy is that young and the whole world seems open to him he does not like to stay in bed long. So, I adopted the system of eating a light breakfast and then a very light lunch. Sometimes I don't eat anything in the middle of the day. With an empty stomach—or partially empty—speed comes naturally. I suppose you who are hunters know what it means to feed a bird dog a heavy meal, in the middle of the day. He simply won't work well that afternoon because he can't.

The gnawing of hunger is a hard thing to overcome. I'll admit that. Still, if an athlete will take something like a plate of soup or a salad sandwich he will have enough in his stomach and not be bothered with hunger until after the ball game. While most athletes have to learn this themselves, others can be trained into it. I agree with Leidy, though, that there are some who will never learn, or rather, who will never have the force of character to deny themselves anything. Only last season I was under the grandstand and saw a ball player—a veteran, too—eat five hot dogs and drink two bottles of sarsaparilla. We tried our hardest to hit balls in his direction that afternoon but luck was against us. I know he must have been as heavy as lead, but luckily for him, he got away with it

This thing of regulating the hours of eating and the amount of food is so important to me that I have tried to instill it into my club. We made quite a success of it down at Augusta two years ago by leasing two of the old homes and running our own boarding house.

By eating like a big family we were able to regulate the food. Most important, though, I was able to tell how the men acted under this system. They seemed to enjoy it. When we left Augusta our club was in wonderful shape to start the season.

The freedom of a big hotel and the carte blanche privileges of the restaurants are enough to tempt any young ballplayer, especially one who has never lived away from home before. Not only is he hungry, but he has a curiosity to try dishes that he has never seen before.

Clark Griffith still talks about the young pitcher who joined his club years ago and ate himself out of the league.

At that time the old Cadillac Hotel in Detroit was run on the American plan and was noted for the generous portions on its menu. This young pitcher came down to breakfast and ordered as he would have done in his home town hotel, where food is served in dishes that look like canary bathtubs.

When the breakfast finally came it took two waiters to bring it. The veteran who sat at the table with the young fellow could hardly find room for his eggs.

"Say," asked the youngster, looking hungrily at the great silver platters that bore his food. "do they eat this way in the big leagues all the time?"

"Do they?" replied the veteran noted as a kidder. "Why, wait till we get to St. Louis and we'll show you a hotel that is a hotel. That's where they do have eating."

"Gee," observed the young fellow, his eyes aglow, "I certainly hope I make good up here!"

That boy couldn't restrain his appetite and ate himself out of the league.

I really believe that more recruits kick away their chances through overeating than from any other cause.

In the hotels that I stopped at while a young bush leaguer there wasn't much danger of anybody overeating. But there was still a chance when we tackled that popcorn and all the truck that is sold about the ball parks.

This regulation of eating can apply just as well to business men.

Chapter 9

"I began to find myself"

I have often wondered if the fans who sit in a grandstand and applaud a great ball player think that he was born that way; that his bunting, throwing and base running came naturally. And I have also wondered if those fans, who laugh at the efforts of a recruit, have any idea of the conflicting thoughts and emotions that are running through his brain.

I have lived through both experiences and I never wonder nowadays at the natural gifts of some great business man or lawyer. I know that his ability and polish were not born in him. I know that he had to learn every bit of it, one detail at a time and that he had to concentrate his whole intelligence and strength on the learning. Men are not born with a grasp of intellectual or physical undertakings. Some men are born with more muscle and some with more brains than others, it is true, but unless those brains are trained to the mastery of details they are of no great value. Less brains, if well trained can do a better job.

With the Augusta club under George Leidy, I began to find myself. It slowly dawned on me that I didn't know anything about baseball. I knew I could hit the ball and throw it, and that I was fast on the bases. Those qualities, however, were merely my tools. I had to learn to use them intelligently. If I hadn't discovered these faults, Leidy would soon have informed me.

Right here I want to give that man credit for starting me out right. He put the right notions into my head and his kindliness kept me working to look well in his eye. He constantly encouraged me and spurred me on.

Up to that time, I had been running hog wild all over the field. I was a bundle of springs—what ball players call a "hustler." I guess I was endowed with more than normal energy. The outlet was on the ball field.

I would run bases harum scarum and would gallop all over the field trying to get into every play. If I caught the ball, I wanted to throw it immediately.

In some ways my speed and energy were a handicap. I would frequently muss things up. Some of the more conservative players wanted to bottle me up. Leidy had a different viewpoint. His years in baseball had given him a clearer vision.

"Boy," he said to me one day, "you got great speed, but you've got to learn to use it. Did you ever try much bunting?"

"You could make many more hits if you could use that speed with a good bunt," Leidy went on. "I'll help you."

That kindly old manager took me out the next morning all by myself. There were no other players to help. Carefully and painstakingly he coached me in the principle of dropping the ball either in the direction of first base or third base and starting to run with the swing of the bat. I saw the point right away.

But I was not a good bunter. I had to learn it by constant practice.

Despite his being past the player age, Leidy would get a glove and field every bunt I hit. Then he would pitch the ball back to me. Often we kept this up for a solid hour. It must have been tiring on him, but he never complained.

"I'll make a ball player out of you yet," he would say laughingly.

I can't imagine many men going through what that old manager did just to help a young kid. Day after day, as regularly as clockwork, he would put on a uniform and go out to the park with me long after the regular players had given up morning practice. Out there we would work and work.

Finally, I got to be a pretty fair bunter. Toward the end of the season, I was surprising opposing pitchers often by dropping the ball and beating it to first. Pick out any successful ball player and you will find that he went through the same thing. That's why I say those qualities are not born in anybody. They've got to learn them, and the only way it can be done is by hard work.

I'll bet you right now that Mr. Harriman worked just as hard on learning the little tricks of railroading as I did on mastering that bunt.°

Another thing that an outfielder must learn by hard knocks is how and when to throw the ball into the field and just at what spot to aim. That may sound like a small matter to you as a fan. To ball players it is all important.

You have heard and I have read of a recruit going into a league game the first time and being cool as ice. There is no such thing—if they are human. Most of them are scared to death. Everything is confused in their minds.

If you ever have been called upon to speak in public in a crowd of, say, a thousand people for the first time, you will have an idea of the feeling that comes over a young ball player on his first appearance. You are pretty badly scared, and you can not remember what you had to say in that speech. Now, imagine yourself appearing before five thousand people, every man of them regarding you critically, and newspapermen ready to give the verdict.

On my first appearance in the field before a crowd, the infielders looked to me to be far away, like statues. It seemed perfectly natural to throw the ball among them, and that one of them would get it. That mental attitude is what causes young fellows to make so many crazy throws. Once they get settled down and have the presence of mind to pick out a certain infielder for a target he seems to get larger.

Anyone can throw to the right man if there is no crowd watch-

---

° EDITOR'S NOTE: Edward Henry Harriman, 1848–1909, controlled the Southern Pacific and the Central Pacific Railroads; father of Averill Harriman. He organized the Northern Securities Company with James J. Hill and J. P. Morgan as a holding company to prevent railroad competition. In 1904 the U.S. Supreme Court dissolved this trust. Harriman was very well known at the time as a tycoon who used his financial strength to buy widely and speculatively in railroad stocks throughout the country.

ing. But that trick of accurate pegging must be learned in public. It is entirely different. Don't think that the young player is
not conscious of being watched.

I remember when I first joined the Detroit club we had a big
pitcher, Willett, who afterward became a success. This day the
big fellow was pitching his first game in the big league and getting away fairly well.

"How does it feel out there," some of the veteran players
asked him.

Willett was a tricky fellow, with no sense of kidding. He spoke
candidly what was in his mind.

"Why," he said, "everything seems to be going all right. I feel
good but somehow I just can't keep my knees from shaking. It
bothers me. How do you stop that?" he asked Bill Donovan.
"Do you have it?"

Ty Cobb at age 12 with his first organized baseball team, the Royston Rompers. Ty is in the front row at the far left. *Courtesy: Baseball Magazine*

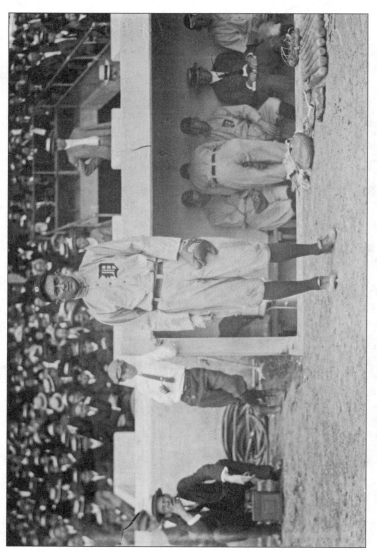

Ty Cobb stands at the dugout before a game in 1913. The 1913 season was a difficult one for Ty, with illness and numerous injuries limiting his play to only 122 games. Still, in 428 trips to the plate he batted .390, which won him the American League batting title for the seventh consecutive time. *Courtesy: Library of Congress, Bain Collection*

Chapter 10

"Being watched by keen eyes"

Probably the greatest initial thrill that any young ball player enjoys is when he discovers that big league scouts are on his trail. To him it means that he has begun to climb the ladder. It is the same thrill that comes to a second lieutenant in the army when he learns that his name is up for promotion.

At the same time it is an uncomfortable feeling to realize that every little movement you make on the field is being watched by keen eyes.

It was late in 1905 when I was tipped off that two scouts were following our club to look at me. I imagine George Leidy, always interested in my future, had told them about me.

The first real scout I ever saw was Harry Vaughan, then manager of the Birmingham club of the Southern League, and formerly a big league catcher for the Cincinnati Reds. He was a man of tremendous size and that impressed me as symbolic of major leagues.

Our club went on a trip to Jacksonville. and there I discovered that Heinie Youngman, of the Detroit Club, was also looking me over. I gritted my teeth that day and played my hardest. In a few days I had been sold, Youngman being impressed with my speed and what Leidy had told him of my aggressiveness.

There have been many conflicting statements as to what I cost the Detroit club. In view of what is being paid now the price does seem ridiculous, but it should be remembered that conditions were entirely different then.

For example, after I had been in the big league for two or three years we had what was considered the greatest opening in history. The papers came out with big headlines announcing, "Record Breaking Big League Crowd of 14,000 Sees Tigers Open Season."

Youngman conferred with Pinckney Steiner, of our Augusta Club, and offered $500 for my transfer to Detroit. This was accepted.

Later Bill Armour, manager of Detroit, opened negotiations to have me report at once. If that could be arranged he agreed to pay an additional $200. That also was accepted. So the purchase price was $700.

I heard that there was a misunderstanding about this extra $200, the club having agreed to $500 only and that Armour paid the $200 out of his pocket.

Anyway, I was directed to report to Detroit immediately. It seemed that a brand new world was opening up to me. Mind you I had never been in a big city other than Atlanta or Memphis.

I went North by way of Cincinnati and had to lay over two hours in that city. It was the first big city I had ever been in and I took a trolley ride to look it over. The thing that impressed me was the extensiveness of it—so many houses stringing out mile after mile. I was also struck with the limited chance a single individual would have in such an enormous place.

Arriving in Detroit a secretary, something I had not known in baseball, met me at the train. He took me to a hotel and from there I went to see Manager Armour.

First impressions are always lasting. I felt immediately that Armour was a man who would become personally interested in a person. Though his words were few, I listened intently to what he said and never forgot it. All he did was to make me feel at home and to inform me that he was going to give me a chance right away.

"Get on a uniform and be on the bench this afternoon," he said.

I didn't realize it then but I was in for the hardest struggle of my life. Had I known what I was about to face, things might have been different. But I met every obstacle as it came. It was not so easy to win a place on a big league team then as it is now. For that reason I believe we had greater ballplayers then in proportion to the number engaged. The glances of the players as I went to the bench were not unfriendly, but they were decidedly impersonal.

No particular interest was taken in my presence. I had a feeling of being a spectator.

It was on August 30, 1905—I'll not forget the day—that Armour told me to get a glove and go out in the field. In the batting order he put me next to Sam Crawford.

The club had no chance for the pennant then so Armour was in a position to experiment. Our opponents were the New York Yanks, and the famous Jack Chesbro, of whom I had read so much, was pitching. Pretty tough spot to set a youngster in, wasn't it? I wasn't quite eighteen years old.

I was ready to fight my way through, though, and wasn't as scared as I expected. In the field that first inning it seemed to me that the infielders were like little pigmies, a long way off. The big grandstand fascinated me. But I was spared having to make a hard fielding play right off.

I came to bat against Chesbro and I was very much like Pitcher Willett, who couldn't stop his knees from shaking during his first big league appearance.

McIntyre and Lindsey were on the bases and I could feel that every eye in the park was glued on my back. I had heard of Chesbro's famous spitball and was watching for it. Always I had a quick eye. I realized also that Chesbro didn't know exactly how he should pitch to me.

The big fellow wound up and shot one over. I didn't know anything about looking them over and watching to get a pitcher in the hole. I knew where that ball was coming and simply took a sock at it.

I hit it squarely on the nose for two bases and scored both runners. I can feel that hit to this day. There is nothing so satisfactory to a ball player as that feel in the arm and wrists when he meets a ball squarely.

That was my start, and I was a happy Georgia boy that night.

Chapter 11

"Everything struck me so serious"

As I have said before, I have never been able to see the humorous side of baseball, even though I can laugh at the reminiscences of others. I was so deadly intent on mastering the game and everything struck me so serious that I failed to develop a baseball sense of humor.

I was never what ball players call a "kidder." In fact I actually did not know what kidding meant before I first broke into the big league. I took it for granted that when a man said anything he meant exactly that.

It was this concentration on my part, I believe, that helped me to get away to a good start, even though I ran into much unpleasantness. The ways of the big league were awfully hard for me to learn.

You may understand this when it is recalled that when I reported to my first manager I took a letter of recommendation from our preacher which related how I had been a regular attendant at Sunday School and was of high moral character. I had an idea, perhaps, that big leagues would be anxious to help a young fellow make good: take a fatherly interest. I was soon disillusioned.

The first disillusionment taught me the trick of sliding. I have been called a vicious slider and have been accused of purposely injuring players. Such were not my intentions, but I had to protect myself and meet roughness with roughness.

In that first game in New York Kid Elberfeld was playing shortstop. Up to that time I had been a fast baserunner but always slid into bases head first. Nobody had told me different. So far, I had been successful, but it was because I had not gone against crafty big leaguers—men like Elberfeld—who knew every angle of the game.

On my first attempt I slid into second head forward. In a flash it seemed that Elberfeld gave me the knee.

Stepping on the bag to receive the ball from the catcher he blocked my slide by coming down on my head with his knee. My forehead and face were shoved into the hard ground and the skin peeled off just above the eyebrows. The clever way in which he did this completely blocked me. When I got to my feet I was much subdued. I had run into a real big leaguer. I realized that he knew much of what I would have to learn.

I made no complaint but walking back to the bench, I began to think. Every time I rubbed my aching head the more I thought. Incidents like that are lost on the fans. The newspaper report merely said, "Cobb out trying to take second."

"That is no way to slide into base," I said to myself. "I'm all wrong. By going in there head first the baseman has all the advantage. Why didn't somebody tell me about that?"

From then on I watched closely. I noted how Elberfeld and other stars went into the bag—feet first, spikes shining.

"By going in that way," I said to myself, "the advantage is with the slider. He is testing the other fellow's nerve. Why let him test mine?"

The next morning I went out and practiced that slide. I soon discovered that by throwing the feet forward and landing on the side of the hips the body would swerve around one side.

"That's how they escape being touched," I decided. "Now, if a runner can figure the throw he can swerve to either side by little a practice."

I talked to Manager Armour and his answers indicated that my deduction had been correct. I didn't wait to be taught how to slide. I went right in and taught myself after watching the others.

In a very short while I was able to get into a bag with all the speed of the veteran. In fact I introduced what was a new slide in baseball. It came to me in an attempt to protect my ankles. I have small ankles and I knew that if I took a long slide and went jamb into the bag I would likely twist my ankle and be out of commission.

So instinct taught me what I regard as an improvement on the old style. Instead of taking the long slide I would run close up to the base and then throw myself forward quickly—a sort of swoop. The force of a quick swoop or dart would swerve my body around more quickly. I would surprise the baseman and get out of his way before he knew it. Expecting a long slide, he would get in my way. In making this slide I ran into several basemen and that is probably the way I got the reputation of being vicious in trying purposely to cut a fellow down. I am not guilty of any such intention.

After Elberfeld had given me the knee and shoved my head into dirt, I figured that, hereafter, I would put the test up to the baseman and have him look out for himself rather than intimidate me.

It is all a case of beating the other fellow to the punch. I still fail to see why I shouldn't make the baseman a little respectful of me, rather than have him make me scared.

Often I have wondered at the many stories of base runners trying to spike a man while nothing is ever said about a baseman stepping on some green youngster's neck. The fans see one and don't see the other. Ball players know, though.

As I write this I have on my desk letters from fans asking for an honest statement as to the men I have purposely spiked. They mention several cases. Many more basemen have been injured by other base runners than me. Why don't they pick on them? Anyway, I will answer in all frankness these questions in my next article.

When the fans know what I had to combat in my first two years they may have a different viewpoint.

Chapter 12

"I am not that kind"

The baseball spike is a dangerous weapon, though it was never intended as such. Its possibilities developed through that never ending struggle to take advantage of everything the game offered.

For those who may not have had a close view, baseball spikes are divided into two parts: one is for the ball of the foot and one for the heel. On these steel plates, triangular in shape, are three blades, nearly an inch in length and curved on the outer edges— which are sharpened like a knife. On each foot there are, therefore, six of these blades. Their purpose is to enable the player to get a grip on the ground to steady him while running or at the bat.

The feet forward slide developed these spikes as weapons to threaten an infielder in touching a runner coming to the base. Training taught the infielders how to make that touch and still not be hurt.

As I have related, I got my lesson the first game I played against New York when I slid into Kid Elberfeld head on. He promptly gave me the knee and shoved my face into the dirt. After that I went feet forward and let the baseman take the chance.

It was easy to learn that a timid baseman would often fail to make the touch through a fear of these glittering spikes. The aggressive base runner, naturally, will take advantage of this fear.

Let me say right here that I have never deliberately injured a man by going at him viciously, though I have often been accused of it. I must be frank, though, and admit that on one or two occasions I have tried to knock a man over. And, on each occasion, I had good cause. It so happened that I failed, but the players whom I went after knew that I intended to get them, and thereafter they laid off taking advantage of me.

It is easy enough to be considered good-natured and magnanimous if a fellow is willing to let the other fellow take advantage of him and get away with it. I am not that kind. From my early boyhood I have fought back with weapons just as strong as those used against me

For example, Kid Elberfeld did not hesitate to give me the knee and drive my face into the ground so that all the skin was peeled off. He did that because I was green and didn't know how to go into a base. Also, he was determined to block me. The whole incentive behind all rough plays is a desire to win. It is rarely malicious.

When I had learned the hook and slide and could go in feet forward, I made up my mind to pay Elberfeld back in his own medicine for having roughed me up. Mind you, I did not complain or holler. I realized that I had paid the penalty for being green.

The first time I had a chance to go into second after that and knew that Elberfeld would cover the bag I threw myself in the air and went after him just as hard as I could. I felt myself a big leaguer now.

My feet collided with his leg and Elberfeld was knocked four or five feet. He failed to touch. That boy was a sportsman. He got up, rubbed himself, looked at me calmly and went back to his position without saying a word.

"Well, you've learned something," his look implied. "You beat me to it that time and I've got nothing to say."

We had many run-ins after that, but both of us took the attitude that if the other tried something and got away with it everything was all right, and there would be no holler coming. After that Elberfeld knew that he could take no easy advantage of me and I knew that I could take none of him. We both understood it and neither ever complained. In fact, I think we had more respect for each other. I know I had every respect for him.

Back in the early days there was much in the papers about my having cut Frank Baker down.

It is true that I bowled him over, but as to doing it deliberately, no such thought ever entered my mind. He was a big fellow and moved a little slowly when I made my slide. He simply failed to get out of the way. Remember, the base runner has a right to the line to a clear view of the base. If the baseman tries to block he does it at his own peril.

I think a ballplayer stupid who does not exert himself to take advantage of every opportunity to win for his team so long as he is in the right both as to rule and to principle.

The players whom I have gone at with the deliberate intention of knocking them out were Hobe Ferris, Lou Criger, Cy Morgan and Dutch Leonard.

Ferris and Criger had tried to get me, and I warned them that if they did it again I would be after them. I knew that if I let them get away with it I would be bullied for a long time. I made up my mind to go into them roughly. As luck would have it I failed on both occasions. I never cut either one of them. I had just cause and was trying. Many a fellow has tried to get me, and I knew at the time. No ball player can afford to let himself be imposed upon.

The pitchers have little chance of getting anybody with their spikes, but they have just as bad a weapon in what we call that "bean ball." I have had many a pitcher try to "bean" me—that is, throw at my head. And I never let one of them get away with it without knowing that he would have to suffer the consequence.

In the old days the habit of "dusting 'em off" was more common than now. That expression originated from a cry from the bench to a pitcher: "Dust him off"—meaning, come so close with the ball as to knock the dust out of his clothes. The object was to intimidate the batter and drive him away from the plate. There are ball players today who would be good batters but for their fear of being dusted off. They back so far away that they cannot reach a ball that is over this plate.

Against these "dusters" I fought back with my spikes. I will relate the two prominent cases in my next article.

Chapter 13

"An individual battle"

Just when I was beginning to go pretty good as a hitter and had played several times against all the clubs in the league, I could tell that the pitchers were trying to locate my weakness. They have a habit, you know, of conferring with each other as soon as they find out what kind of pitching a new batter fails to hit.

When they fail in that the next step often is to try to intimidate the batter by using the "bean ball." Very few of the really great pitchers would resort to this, but there were a few who were adept at it. They could "dust off" a batter and drive him from the plate in a way that appeared purely accidental. They could fool the crowd, and still can, but they can't often fool the batter.

Up there at the plate is an individual battle between him and the pitcher.

In my last chapter I mentioned Dutch Leonard as one of the ball players whom I had threatened with my spikes. I say threatened because I did not actually cut him.

On two or three occasions Leonard had tried to bean me. One time he came so close to hitting me in the head that I had to fall to avoid being hurt. Just the same, I didn't back away from the plate. I looked at him in such a way that he knew what I was thinking.

"All right," I said to myself, "If that is your game I'll play it right back at you." He knew that I meant that when I looked at him.

An outfielder has no chance of throwing at a pitcher and he has less chance of spiking him on the bases. But he must do something or the pitcher will think he is getting away with something and will no longer respect the batter's rights.

I fail to see where it is any worse for a base runner to go in viciously with his spikes than for the pitcher to throw at a man's head or body.

That kind of stuff has got to be paid back in the same coin. The only way to prevent a pitcher having you nervous and timid is to make him nervous and timid. He must know that there is a come-back.

So I made up my mind to get even with Dutch Leonard, even if I had to threaten him with my spikes. Ordinarily you'd think there is no way of doing it. But there is.

On my next appearance at the plate I let Leonard know by my look that he wasn't going to get away with any attempt to "bean me." That is where my knowledge of bunting, as George Leidy taught me, came in.

I realized that the only way to get even with Leonard was to make him cover first base. So I deliberately bunted the ball toward first base. Leonard ran over to cover the bag. It was an easy out, and Leonard was over the bag and in the coach's box when I got within ten feet of it. Just the same I deliberately took the jump. With my feet flying forward and the spikes showing I did not aim at the bag at all but slid right through the coacher's box where Leonard had been standing. I didn't touch him, but I had made the threat.

Leonard knew fully well why I had made that slide through the coacher's box. He knew that I was demonstrating how he could be paid back if he tried to bean me again. It is a game that both could play at if he dusted me off again.

I had no hard feelings against Leonard and I think we are pretty good friends,** but by that one threat I had saved myself

***

** EDITOR'S NOTE: In May 1926, a few months after these memoirs were written, Dutch Leonard accused Ty Cobb, Tris Speaker and Joe Wood of fixing a 1919 game between Cleveland and Detroit, and betting on its outcome. This would lead to the resignations of both Cobb and Speaker, their subsequent release from their manager positions, and their banishment from the

from future bluffing. He didn't try to bean me again. I still think
I was perfectly justified in showing that I also had weapons to
use if it were necessary.

The other pitcher who fought me many a battle on the dia-
monds was Cy Morgan. He also tried to dust me off several
times. In fact, he did succeed in hitting me while I stood at the
bat. I let him know that I was wise to what he was doing and that
I would get even. I had to stop him or they would all be trying
that bean ball. The Boston club, you know, had a reputation for
their pitchers keeping opposing batters away from the plate.

After Morgan had beaned me hard I shook my finger at him
as much as to say he would get his when the first opportunity
arose.

I don't remember exactly who was on base or who hit the ball
but I started in from first on a long hit. As I rounded third,
Morgan, who had run over to cover the plate, was already set to
catch the ball. I had no chance of scoring. He had me before I
was ten feet past third. Just the same I deliberately kept on and
made a long and vicious slide straight at him. A pitcher doesn't
have to take many throws at the plate and does not know how to
block as a catcher does. Anyway, my slide caused Morgan to
step out of the way. I had handed Morgan the same kind of bluff
he had handed me. He knew very well why I had done it, too.

This affair started a feud between Morgan and myself. Just as
often as he tried to bean me I would try to get back at him with
my spikes. On one occasion I tried to bunt one toward first so as
to make him cover the bag. I was just angry enough to go at him
as I had at Dutch Leonard. But to save my life, that day I
couldn't bunt a ball in that direction. The next time the feud was
temporarily forgotten. But it would be renewed every time we
faced each other.

Finally Morgan went to the Athletics, who won the pennant.
As it was five days before the National League season was over

---

American League. Both Cobb and Speaker were publicly cleared by
Kenesaw Landis in January 1927, in time for Cobb to join Connie Mack's
Philadelphia Athletics for the 1927 season.

we went down to play against the Athletics to practice them up for the big series.

Everybody on the Philadelphia club was feeling pretty good, especially Morgan who had been exchanged in time to get a share of the big receipts.

In that practice series Cy and I got together and decided to wipe out the feud. We decided that neither of us were getting the best of it and that neither got the worst of it. But neither had been a quitter.

Chapter 14

"A survival of the fittest"

No ballplayer ever went through any harder struggle or suffered more heavy burning and general unpleasantness than myself in earning a place in the big league. Others have gone through struggles as hard, but none harder.

I do not say this in disparagement of my teammates—there were some wonderful lovable characters among them—but I have given my word that I will be frank and in that spirit I will answer the many inquiries as to why I had so many arguments and fights.

I sincerely believe that I was a much better ballplayer for all those hard knocks. In those days a young fellow had to fight his way through almost insurmountable obstacles—obstruction that the fans never see—to get any kind of a start at all. It was, in other words, a survival of the fittest.

That is why I am convinced that there were more real ball players in proportion to the number engaged than there are today. The game has improved and is on a broader scale, but individual ability has not improved. There are more good ball players now simply because there are more working at the job.

I do not propose to defend myself against the charge of being a belligerent, nagging ball player. I simply nagged back when they nagged me. My own belligerency was merely a defense against belligerency. I never did and never do intend to take the worst of it in open competition unless I have to. If that kind of spirit is reprehensible, then I am guilty.

The first thing that confronted a young ball player back in 1905 was the fact, admitted frankly on the bench, that his success meant knocking some other fellow out of a job. The friends of the other fellow—his teammates—do not like to see him ousted by a young stranger. On every team there was one or more of these young strangers, and what they were up against can be appreciated.

There was not then the general desire among the players to see and help a new player develop, simply because it hurt the chances of some veteran. Nowadays any good man can be taken care of without costing others a job.

Those rough days of hazing are gone. Baseball has grown too big to have patience with it. As a result, the ball player of today is more of a young business man. He enters the game with everybody reaching out to help him. His success makes him a business asset to owners and players. He is not heckled and roughly treated by his teammates. The new player of today comes in at a good salary, plays his game and can enjoy it like any other successful young fellow.

By not having to go through the grind, the hard knocks, these new players, as a rule, have not the ground work and tenacity of such men as Walter Johnson, Clark Griffith, John McGraw, Eddie Collins, Tuck Turner, Napoleon Lajoie or any of that school.

Many a boy with natural ability lost his opportunity in those early days because us teammates made it too hard for him.

When I joined the Detroit club and signed a contract for $1,500 a year I thought I had done a big thing. That seemed like considerable money. I was particularly elated because, at that time, it was rare that a player who had not been in the Class A or Class B minors was accepted in the big league.

As I have said before I got in a game right away and made a two-base hit off Jack Chesbro as a starter. I kept right on hitting pretty well. My fielding was said to be acceptable. Then my trouble started.

The situation was this: Davy Jones had just come in with a big reputation and was sure of his job. Sam Crawford was certainly sure of his. McIntyre had been playing regularly and it looked as if the matter of regular job was between McIntyre and myself. McIntyre, poor fellow, is dead now. I do not blame him personally any more than I would blame others. It was simply a system of which he was part.

Seeing a possibility of me making good the regular players, friends and pals of Matty McIntyre, naturally resented it. They couldn't understand that there was room for us both.

As a result of this, feeling arose against me. Many of the players would not extend me a helping hand. What is more, they set about to haze me and make it generally unpleasant. It was worse than the hazing at college because it lasted longer. I had never understood rough kidding, had never heard some of the language used on a big league bench. At first it actually shocked me. It was unbelievable to me that men could take some of the epithets and be manly. I didn't understand that these things were not meant as insults, were joking terms. I was very unhappy.

I must say, though, that Manager Bill Armour acted as father to me and gave me every help possible. He had made up his mind to "launch" me and he stuck to it. He forgave my faults: at any rate he pointed them out and helped me correct them.

The first harshness came when McIntyre told me one day that I couldn't take my batting turn with the regulars in practice. Others shoved me aside the same way.

"Go out there in the field where you belong and shag fly balls," they told me.

That method of putting a young fellow in his place, by the way, was a common form of harassing. I thought that they meant exactly what they said and I felt badly. I went to Bobby Lowe and asked him if it was true that I was not allowed to take my batting turn. Then I went to Armour.

"Go up there and take your turn," they told me. "If they say anything shove 'em out of the way. They're kidding you."

I was boiling at this. But, with the encouragement, I walked up ready to fight for my rights. Despite their looks I took my turn.

My next discovery was a tragedy. I found that somebody had broken my bats and thrown parts of them away.

Matty McIntyre was the Detroit center fielder in 1905 whose position was challenged by the 18 year old newcomer, Ty Cobb. McIntyre led the group of Cobb's teammates who harassed and hazed the young Ty Cobb. By 1907, the first complete season that Ty Cobb played, McIntyre played in only 20 games. He later was traded to the Chicago White Sox, where he finished his career. *Courtesy: Library of Congress, Bain Collection*

Hughie Jennings was a standout shortstop for the old Baltimore Orioles from 1893 to 1899. In 1907 he was hired to manage the Detroit Tigers, when Ty Cobb was first being recognized as a baseball prodigy. Jennings gave Ty Cobb free reign to manage himself, and thereby led the Tigers to three straight American League pennants (1907-1909). He managed the Tigers, and Ty Cobb, for 14 seasons, until Cobb took over the manager position in 1921. He was elected to the Hall of Fame in 1945. *Courtesy: Library of Congress, Bain Collection*

Chapter 15

"A lot of encouragement"

The narration of my early difficulties in baseball—my personal difficulties—is not a pleasant task. I had rather not think of it. Still, if it helps to point out the trials of a young ball player, or any other young man, it may be worth while.

I am not one of those who regard a fiery temper always as a handicap. Take my own case. If I had been easy going and had not fought back, the chances are I would not be in a position to tell this story of a long experience in baseball.

When the hazing players would get me angry and upset by some petty act, I often have gritted my teeth and declared to myself that I would get a base hit the next time up or die in the attempt. A good clean hit and dash down first always did more to relieve my feelings than any one thing.

One day just as the newspapers were printing stories about my hitting I started to bat and found that not one of my favorite sticks was in the bag. I was all broken up. I had to use another bat.

"I'd like to find the man who took my bats," I remarked, hotheaded, as I came back to the bench. There was no response.

I looked around as if to find a friendly face.

A little later Bill Donovan, God rest his good soul, called me me aside.

"Kid," he said to me, "don't think that you haven't a friend on this ball club. The fellows may razz you and pull that bush stuff,

51

but there are some here who are your friends and who are going to see that you get an even break.

"I am your friend and whenever you need a friend call on me. I'll see that you can get an even break anytime you start. Don't let these fellows keep you from being a good ball player."

An older man rarely ever realizes what a few words like that mean to a youngster. But those words of Old Bill sunk into me. I gritted my teeth and worked all the harder. Manager Armour and Bobby Lowe also proved themselves my friends and gave me a lot of encouragement.

The whole trouble was that a few of McIntyre's friends had sort of formed a gang which kept aloof from me. They clearly made me feel my position—that as a recruit I had no place in their counsels. I had to go about alone.

Then they used to take my hat off the rack in the hotel and twist it out of shape, leaving it that way for me to pick up. But I was always looking for the guilty man, and if we got together it was a fight. There was nothing humorous in all this to me. Because I was fiery-tempered and willing to fight I think they did much of this just to spur me on.

The impression had gone around that Charlie Schmidt, the catcher, was my bitterest enemy. That is not true. A long time ago Charlie came to me and told me he was sorry for all those mix-ups and that often the players had dared him to go out and pull something on me.

It was with Schmidt that I had my first fight. It arose over some trivial incident on the bench. He was a much bigger man than I, but we mixed it up. In the struggle he fell over a barrel and I pounced on top of him as he lay on the barrel. They pulled us apart, but the felling had started.

Sometime later the gang had been roasting Schmidt and as I turned around the corner of the bench he soaked me a hard one right on the jaw. There wasn't any fight about that. I simply hit the ground.

I also had a fight with Siever, the pitcher. He also is dead now, poor fellow. But he and I made up and became good friends.

It seems the gang had ribbed him up with some story to go

after me because of a ground ball being missed in the field while
he was pitching. I didn't know this and was standing at the cigar
counter in the old Southern Hotel in St. Louis, buying some
chewing gum. Siever, leaving the gang, came over to where I
was standing. Just as he walked up Bill Donovan stepped
between us and putting his hand on the counter, said, "Now,
don't have any trouble here, fellows.'

I hadn't heard of any trouble and that put me wise. I wanted
to find out more. A little later I was leaning against one of the
big columns all alone when Siever again left the crowd and came
over to me. As he came around the post he swung his left at me.
I was lucky. In swinging his left—he was a southpaw—he left his
jaw open and I took a crack at it and landed. I didn't get the
worst of that fight, but it didn't add to my popularity with the
gang.

The feeling extended to the field, and it got to where I felt
that McIntyre wasn't backing me up.

It had come to a showdown when a long drive was hit closer
to him than to me. We were both stubborn and stood our
ground. The ball went through for a home run. Finally McIntyre
had to go and get it. The crowd—a St. Louis crowd—gave us a
terrible razzing. When McIntyre came to the bench, the players
roasted him and when I got there a little later they also roasted
me.

I happened to restore myself partly by getting a two-base hit
my next time up.

This incident really helped to end all the foolishness. The
leading players, seeing that the hazing feeling was affecting the
playing, decided it best to lay off. After that I never had a great
deal of trouble.

Chapter 16

"To drive the machine"

The two main qualities required in a baseball manager are: First, an ability to discover potential greatness in young players and to build them up as individuals and, second, an ability to handle and direct the players as a collective group—to drive the machine, in other words.

It is rarely a man possesses both of these qualities in high degree.

This is written in answer to a letter from a Detroit fan, asking my opinion in managers with whom I have been associated.

I had an unusual opportunity to get a clear idea of this when I first broke in and after I had been successful enough to lead the league in batting.

Bill Armour, manager of the Detroit club, who bought me from Augusta and gave me my start, was a distinct type of the man who understands the individual merits in a player and could develop them. He was a wonder at launching new players. The proper "launching" of a player is a mighty important event and has to be carefully studied by the manager.

If you will look back to those days it will be seen that Armour developed many of the players who became stars in the great machine to be led by Hughie Jennings. But somehow Armour could not handle the team so well as a group. He concentrated his attention on the individuals.

When Hughie Jennings came to Detroit as manager, relieving

Armour, the machine really began to work in co-ordination. He was helped immensely at the start by having the benefit of the training work already done by Armour.

It was very much like the training of soldiers for the World's War. Often it happened that the man who had collected these soldiers and taught them the rudiments was unable to lead them in battle. Jennings came on as a born field leader, a real general, who led the club to greatness.

It would be difficult to say which deserves greater credit. It is certain, however, that the man who wins a pennant lasts longer in the memory. Personally I have a downright affection for both those men, and as I got my first impression of big league baseball from watching them I can never forget the great qualities of both.

Jennings was a natural and an intelligent leader. He knew the trick of centering his strength at the right spot. He had another great quality in encouraging the players to work together for the common good. The men played their heads off without realizing that they were being directed by an astute and kindly man.

Possession of the two managerial qualities I have mentioned, I discovered, was always the big problem. Managers themselves realize that they can handle a machine better if they have somebody else recruit its strength. It is almost impossible for one man to think for his group on the field and at the same time attend to the worries of bringing out some one youngster. If he can he is one of the truly great.

The practice of trading players grew into popularity because of many managers being unwilling and unable to give up their time to constructive work while trying to win a pennant. It is much easier to go out and buy an experienced ball player to fill a certain job than it is to train one for the job. Men in big business understand that principle. It is cheaper, for example, to engage an experienced salesman at high price than to risk breaking in a youngster who has been waiting for a chance.

Even the big newspapers of this country would hesitate to send a cub reporter to cover a national convention. Baseball has grown into such an important business that a manager cannot lightly risk the loss of a pennant by making experiments. An experienced player who can join a team and become the necessary cog to win a championship is worth almost anything that may be paid for him.

When you hear that such and such a manager is a great field leader but is not constructive don't blame him too much. There is always a reason why he can't devote his mind to both branches at the same time. He is judged by the pennant he wins or the drawing power of his club. The development of young players is forgotten if he does win.

There have been a few great managers who were able to build and lead at the same time, but very few. Connie Mack is a notable example. Even his field leadership could not pull him through when he broke up his great team and started to build anew.

I don't know so much about John McGraw personally. But he must possess both of those great qualities. His great record in winning so many pennants is evidence of that.

It has been said that some managers do not deserve so much credit because they were in positions to buy a player whenever they felt like it and that the price did not count. Think that over a moment and you will find that the manager had to build his club into a popular winning machine before he could exercise that power.

I think one of the best instances of field leadership I ever saw was that of Stanley Harris in the world's series of 1924. He had several wise old veterans to help him, but he was put in a position of having to lead these older men and blend their efforts so as to bring out every ounce of strength.

During the season Harris's mind was concentrated on his own play at second base and at the bat—enough for any man ordinarily. Still, Harris had such perfect mental poise and balance that he could think for the whole club while trying to go through with his own individual work. In the midst of a critical play in which he was involved he was able to stop and make changes that threw fresh strength into the fight. I doubt that the general public realizes just how wonderful was the work of Harris that first year as manager. He proved his ability as a leader by nursing his club along to a second pennant even though he did fail to win another world series.

Harris is a great field leader. The coming season will decide whether he has that other qualification of building up youngsters to keep his machine balanced on the same high plane.

Chapter 17

"The game runs in cycles"

Did it ever occur to you fans who have watched baseball for twenty years or more that the game runs in cycles? Did you ever notice that the points most strongly stressed a few years ago have passed out and are now out of style?

The struggle to keep up with the styles or fads in playing baseball is almost as constant as that of the ladies in finding what is being worn in Paris.

For example, the game is right now in the slugging cycle. Every batter is trying to make home runs. A few years ago it was the place hit. But to be in the limelight these days a batter must make home runs, and a lot of them. A few years ago a batter would have been fined for swinging as they do nowadays.

The next cycle I think will be one of psychology. I can see it coming on—but that's ahead of my story. It's a subject that I will take up later.

The first cycle that I remember was the overhand pitching. It was believed that no man could possibly make his mark unless he had a perfect overhand motion, like that of Bill Donovan or Christy Mathewson. But that idea was knocked sky-high by the underhand pitching of men like Carl Mays.

The next cycle was when the whole game went crazy over the idea of the hit and run; the perfection of hitting behind the runner and so on. Then came a cycle of base stealing.

To me the most interesting because of its temporary nature

was the great cycle of the famous trick balls. Every pitcher in the land was sitting up at night thinking up ways of doing tricky things to the ball. This came right on the heels of the hullabaloo over the spitball. Most of those pitchers, too, were really clever inventors. They got away with the most astonishing tricks, some of which have not been solved or exposed to this day. A rule was adopted to do away with all freak pitching, but it still crops out in spots. Every once in a while we catch a fellow pulling some freak stunt. Much of it has never been exposed.

For instance, nobody knows to this day—not even his own manager and the coaches—what it was that Eddie Cicotte did to a ball to make it sail in that peculiar manner so completely puzzling to batters.

The most prominent of the trick balls were the emery ball, the sailer, the knuckle ball and the raised seam ball; there were others, though.

The cycle of freak pitching was at its height soon after I came in—just when I was beginning to get up among the leaders as a batter.

In New York one day I was surprised to learn that not one of the players nor the owners of the present American League team, the Yanks, was familiar with sleight of hand work of Russell Ford, former New York pitcher, that upset the whole league for two seasons.

Ford, a most intelligent fellow, had an odd delivery that was almost unhittable. He had overhand swing that was noticeably good and his form was not up to that of the really great pitchers. Still he would send a ball up at the batter that would suddenly dart away. It was almost impossible to get hold of it. We tried every way we knew of finding his secret, but to no avail. We knew that he did something unusual to the ball, but we couldn't get a clue. We called it the emery ball because we often found a side of it roughed up as if rubbed with emery paper. But one day when his clothes were searched it was found that Ford carried no emery paper.

It was years before anybody learned how Ford managed to apply this emery and how he made the original discovery.

Russell Ford was pitching at Atlanta one day when a wild

pitch went over Catcher Sweeney's head and struck a concrete post. This roughed up one side of the ball. On the next pitch Sweeney noticed that the ball took a peculiar shoot and almost got away from him.

"What is that you are throwing?" he asked Ford. "It jumped a half foot."

Ford himself didn't know exactly, but he began studying this odd phenomenon.

After many experiments he reached the conclusion that the roughed side of the ball caught the wind and the friction gave the ball a lopsided motion, causing it to veer off from a straight course at odd angles. Sweeney was prepared for it that time. Ford at that time used a piece of emery paper to scrape the ball, the paper being concealed in his pocket.

Ford was unhittable. In time the other players began to investigate. They knew that Ford was roughing off the ball, but didn't know the method. The pitchers were thereafter forbidden to carry anything in their pockets. Still Ford kept on pitching that puzzling ball.

News of this got around and the New York club bought Ford.

When he was engaged, though, it was learned that Sweeney alone knew the secret and neither he nor Ford would tell anybody else. So, to be sure the New York club also purchased Sweeney in order to keep the combination. I am told that is how Sweeney got in the big leagues.

Ford and Sweeney were just as successful with their secret in the big league as in the minors. It was two years before we learned the trick.

Russell Ford always wore a ring while pitching and he and Sweeney conceived the idea of having this ring made of emery. As a darkly mounted ring it did not attract unusual attention and nobody suspected its real purpose.

As he started to pitch Ford would bring the emery to bear on the ball and work it around until he had roughed up a spot about the size of a half of a dollar. He also experimented until he knew which way the ball would shoot, and communicated it to Sweeney. Between them they kept the secret inviolate.

For two years this mystery remained. Then Kahler of Cleveland, having learned the trick some way in the minors, came up with it. Next, Falkenberg got it.

About that time the big league batters began to understand. They would complain and have the roughed ball thrown out. But just as they were feeling easier Eddie Cicotte bobbed up with a sailing ball, the secret of which has not been discovered to this day. The other trick balls I will discuss in the next article.

Chapter 18

"The style of trick pitching"

While the development of trick ball pitching was not a good thing for baseball, the inventors of those mysterious devices for fooling batters are really entitled to more credit than they ever received. As geniuses they ranked with the magicians like Hermann the Great°°° and Houdini. Their art was lost to the public, though, because the fans had no way of knowing what was going on.

When the emery ball secret of Russell Ford and others was laid bare that delivery was promptly abolished but others existed and still exist, for that matter.

Eddie Cicotte's great success was due almost entirely to his "sailor." This ball would start like an ordinary pitch and then would sail much in the manner of a flat stone thrown by a small boy. The ball didn't take much of a jump but just enough to keep a batter from getting hold of it. Nobody, not even his own catcher, ever knew just what Cicotte did to the ball. Kid Gleason, his manager and other members of the White Sox tried in vain to discover the secret, but Cicotte never divulged it. When he was thrown out of organized baseball his secret went with him.

°°° EDITOR'S NOTE: Alexander Hermann, d. 1896, the first in a succession of Grand Masters of The Royal Dynasty of Magic, was America's Premier Magician in the late 19th century.

The umpires could never catch him doing anything illegal. Still, we all knew that he did.

Cicotte was so adept that all he asked was for the ball to be rolled to him on the ground. With a brand new ball that had not touched the dirt he couldn't deliver the sailor. But that was quickly arranged by the catcher and the infielders rolling the ball to him on the ground. From then on the batters were ducking around to avoid that puzzling sailor.

Sothoron came next, with a trick ball that acted very much like the emery ball of Russell Ford. In time his secret was discovered but before we had done so he had made a great record. He worked it by raising a corrugation on the side of the ball without the aid of any foreign substance. By the use of a strong forefinger and thumb Sothoron would work up the seam of the ball until it stood out.

This slight raise or corrugation on the surface was enough to catch the wind and cause the ball to take the queer swerves and shoots. In his case, great accuracy was required in handling the ball so that the seam would catch the air at the right time. He could actually control the ball.

One of the greatest artists of the whole lot was Dave Danforth. To this day opposing batters take scrupulous care about every ball that he pitches. Fans often make fun of the catcher in demanding to be shown the ball. They think it a way of killing time. Rather than take any chances the umpire often throws the ball out even when he does not see anything wrong.

If you will remember, poor Ray Chapman was killed by a ball that took a quick jump. Carl Mays had not intended using a trick ball but the ball had got "feathers," that is roughed up by contact with the hard dirt. Just before that pitch the catcher had requested that the ball be thrown out. But it seemed perfectly all right.

In the case of Dave Danforth it was found that he used paraffin on the seam of the ball, making it appear perfectly smooth and legal. He and others discovered that by delicately slitting the little raised places between the stitches in the seam a raised edge could be had whenever desired. These slits were made with a safety razor blade. Then the seam was pressed back into place, covered with paraffin and rubbed in. There was absolutely nothing to show that the ball had been tampered with.

But when the pitcher wanted to raise a surface on the ball all he had to do was scrape away the paraffin with his thumbnail and bring up the slit edges. This raised edge, being a part of the seam, would escape notice and would be even more effective as a windbreak than a patch roughed up by emery paper.

Without doubt there are still instances of a pitcher using trick deliveries but they are not so frequent.

These tricks that are done by changing the surface of the ball must not be confused with such things as the knuckle ball. That was a legal delivery but very difficult to operate. The ball was balanced between the thumb and the little finger with the other fingers doubled up so that the ball would take its momentum from the knuckle. That never became general because it was not practical. A pitcher who can control a ball that way is certainly entitled to the privilege.

While Christy Mathewson never even used the spitball much there is no doubt but that he could have done so had he desired. He thought it hurt the arm and that the straight over-hand delivery was more generally effective. Bill Donovan took a similar view.

Just to amuse himself Matty discovered an odd "floater" that could be developed from a semi-use of the spitter. He used to amuse the catchers with it in practice but he never attempted it in game.

I forgot to say in discussing Russell Ford that he kept his secret a long time by pretending he was pitching a spitter. He would deliberately show his finger to the batter and then wet it with saliva. This covered up his real trick of using the emery finger-ring to rough the ball.

But the cycle of trick pitching has ended. Our next one, I think, will be psychology. Later I will show why I think so.

Chapter 19

"Attack at those weaknesses"

I am quite sure that a big factor in what success I may have had in baseball has been due to an instinctive study of psychology on my part. I did not know it by that name when I started, but it was always natural with me to try to study the workings of the other fellow's mind, especially an opponent's.

I have found that if a man is able to analyze himself he is pretty apt to be proficient in analyzing others. When I began to discover my own weaknesses I could discover them in others. Then it was easy to aim my attack at those weaknesses.

A man can get along with a lot less natural ability if he knows what to aim it at, and when to shoot. Nearly all ball players have mannerisms or habits and when these are upset it throws them all out of gear.

Our ball club got to where we could beat Carl Mays, the great underhand pitcher, most any time he started, and fans often wondered why. We did it because we had studied his way of thinking, and crossed him.

It is well known among batters that Mays's great point of strength was in his low ball. He keeps it just about the knees and worries a batter to death. But he always manages to keep it high enough for the umpire to call a strike.

We discovered one day that if Mays couldn't control his low ball he lost his poise and was easy to beat. His mind was in such habit of having that low one—his strength—work successfully that when it didn't his grip was gone.

After watching him closely I found that he sized up batters according to where they stood in the batter's box. As you may know, I usually stand well forward and meet the ball out in front. By pitching to me in that position Mays's low ball would come just above my knees. The next time up I stood far back in the box, which put me a yard farther away from him. His low ball came over as usual, but when it reached the back end of the box it was an inch or two below my knees.

The umpire called two balls and Mays was surprised. Something was wrong, but he couldn't understand. I knew, of course, he would have to steady himself and get the next one up. Instead of waiting, I swung on that one and got a hit.

One after another of our batters tried the scheme and we drove Mays from the box. After that we could beat him most any time we wanted to by staying in the back of the box. That shifting completely upset him.

A similar scheme, but in a different way, helped us to beat Urban Shocker. He was always a puzzler to us until we discovered that his strong point was his high ball. He had a tantalizing way of keeping that just around the shoulders so that it would be called a strike and still would be very difficult to hit.

After a conference on the bench we decided for the long hitters who stood in the back of the box to move forward as far as possible. Those who already stood that way would lean forward as he pitched so that their body would really be over the forward edge of the box.

All of a sudden Shocker discovered that he had lost control, and he couldn't tell how. By standing up so close his high ball, pitched as he usually pitched it, would pass up two inches or higher and would be called a ball. Finding that his main point of strength was missing, Shocker was upset.

In desperation he would bring the ball down lower to have it called a strike and, without waiting, we would sock it. In other words, when we challenged a man's strength until he found it really a weakness, we had him on the defensive. That is all a batter needs. Once the pitcher is on the defensive he is licked.

The most striking instance of psychology that I remember

having seen was in the world's series between the Giants and the Athletics back in 1911.

Chief Bender, the Indian, one of baseball's keenest students worked the psychology on Chief Meyers, also an Indian, the heavy hitter of the Giants.

Now, everybody knew that Meyers could literally kill a fast ball, and he knew that speed was Bender's long suit.

"Don't pitch him a fast one," the Athletics kept yelling to Bender from the bench.

As the two Indians faced each other Bender finally got two strikes on Meyers. If I remember correctly, they were on fouls. Now Meyers knew that Bender wouldn't dare pitch him a fast one after that, and Bender doped it out that Meyers was thinking exactly that way.

So Bender deliberately and very obviously motioned for all the fielders to move around toward right, indicating to a ball player that he was going to pitch a curve and would pull it in that direction. He then went so far as to hold a conference and make it clearer to Meyers's mind just what he intended to do. After letting this sink in until Chief Meyers was all set for a curve, Bender walked back to the box.

Taking a big windup, Bender cut loose a fast one with the speed of a bullet. It cut the plate squarely in the middle. Meyers, being so sure of a curve, was dumbfounded. He was crossed so completely that he couldn't even swing at the ball.

Chapter 20

"The eye is quicker than the hand"

M y greatest moment of personal satisfaction in baseball—of achievement—was when I first won the batting championship in the American League. That had been my goal for several years. My ambition had been concentrated on it. I had studied and analyzed everything pertaining to the art of batting that my rather youthful mind could grasp. I was immensely elated when my name headed the list.

Very soon thereafter I was asked to prepare an article on the art of batting for the benefit of college boys and other amateurs. Since I began writing these memoirs I have been asked again to write something on batting that will help the young boys.

I don't want to pose as a sage or a know-it-all, but after fifteen years I find little to add to my impressions which I so laboriously put down at that time.

I wrote then:°°°° "The eye is the main factor in batting and the boy who is ambitious to become a good batter will see to it that his optic nerve is trained. The eye is quicker than the hand, a truism that finds more proof in baseball than in any other form of activity.

There are few boys or even veteran big leaguers who do not

°°°° EDITOR'S NOTE: There was no close quote within the original published Chapter 20. Thus, it is not known precisely how much of this chapter was quoted from the earlier article on batting written by Ty Cobb.

show more enthusiasm in swinging the bat than in any other department of the game. Even if a player is not to play in a game, he will insist on having his turn at bat in practice. The sheer delight of smacking the ball keeps him interested. It is always great fun to bat, even in the back yard.

There is much more in batting than a youngster imagines. It requires study—hard and persistent study. In all this the eye plays the most important part. Unless it is trained to be keen, no boy may hope to become a good batter. He must take good care of his eyes at all times. This means that the eyes must not be strained by overwork such as reading under a bad light or while lying in an awkward position. No good batter will read in bed at night.

Why, Pie Traynor, the hard-hitting third baseman of the Pittsburgh Pirates, won't even go to a moving picture during the season for fear of it affecting his eyes.

The most common source of injury to the nerves of the eye is cigarette smoking. Next to it is the use of alcoholic liquors. The latter is not so common. Few good ball players drink, while many of them—most of them, in fact—insist upon smoking cigarettes. But if the player goes too far the cigarette smoke is sure to ruin his batting eye sooner or later. Whenever you start out in the morning with a sort of haze before the eye or when you see those little spots right after breakfast it is usually the fault of cigarettes. Cigarette smoking also affects the wind, but that is another subject.

Some boys are born with naturally good eyesight. It is possible for those less fortunate to develop theirs. Once they do, it is a great baseball asset.

Handball is perhaps the best developer of the eye. In this game the eye is quickly trained to follow an object swiftly, and to give quick command to the hand. Learning to see in a flash or to follow any rapidly moving object is a great help in batting.

To the young batter—and the old—I would say keep your eye glued on the pitcher and watch his hand until the ball leaves it. Don't let your glance waver, or you are gone. Keep your eye on the ball on its journey to the plate. If you have tried training the eye at handball, for instance, you will soon find yourself able to judge accurately the speed of a ball leaving a pitcher's hand. That is the whole trick. Curves won't bother you much if you are a perfect judge of speed.

Now, when you take your position at the bat, stand naturally; the way that seems most comfortable to you. Taking a good stance in baseball is just as important as in golf. The position of the feet and the ease with which you can pivot the body means everything. The important thing is to acquire rhythm.

The trouble with a lot of batters is that they assume unnatural, awkward positions. Be at ease. If you don't feel right, step out of the box and try it again. Don't be in a hurry. The pitcher will have to wait. He will certainly take his time about getting ready. So don't let him get on your nerves. Remember that when you are ill at ease or uncomfortable that there is something wrong and that it will take part of your mind off the approaching ball.

Once you find yourself at ease, however, stand there and wait for a good ball. The first good one that comes along, step out well in front of the plate and get your bat on the ball before the curve breaks. Keep as far forward as possible. Many boys and men imagine that they can see the ball better if they stand far back in the box. That is common tendency among young batters. It is entirely wrong.

Remember that the pitcher depends upon the breaking of his curve ball and the jump of his fast one to fool you. By stepping toward him you can rob him of this advantage. In other words, the trick of batting is to play the ball instead of letting it play you. Be on the offensive. Never allow yourself to be put on the defensive at the bat, in the field, on the bases or in any walk of life.

The aggressive, positive men win the prizes of life. The negative, defensive men usually pay the freight. Why not train yourself to be a winner?

Now, another thing—never try to place a hit. In the first place, you can't do it, and it is not a good idea, anyway. Very few batters ever successfully acquired the art. I never try to place hit. I have tried simply to meet the ball solidly and let the hits find holes for themselves. They usually will. Most boys have an idea that when the infielders or outfielders spread apart, and leave a wide gap, that they can hit the ball right through the gap. Don't fool yourself that way. By centering your mind on that open spot you are taking it off the ball. As a result you either strike out or pop up a fly. It is like the golfer who tries to see where the ball is going before he hits it. Your job should be to hit the ball on the nose, that's all.

Chapter 21

"Hit the ball on the nose"

In my preceding article on the art of batting I tried to impress upon young batters—old ones, too, for that matter—the futility of trying to place hits instead of merely concentrating the mind and muscles on hitting the ball on the nose. That can not be over-emphasized. Before I elaborate let me repeat to the ambitious batter:

Take care of your eyes at all times by not straining them under a bad light or by excessive cigarette smoking. Then learn to get a comfortable position in the batter's box and center your mind on merely meeting the ball squarely. The rest will take care of itself.

It may be difficult for some of you young ball players to get back to those simple principles because you probably have been trying something more technical and tricky. There are many tricks in batting, it is true, but you can learn those after you have developed a good swing and an ability to hit the ball on the nose. Don't forget that when you try to place a hit you are thinking of that instead of hitting the ball. So, don't do it.

As you progress you will learn that the first important sidelight on the art of batting is the "working" of the pitcher. In the big league it is necessary to "work" or worry the pitcher if you hope have any big advantage. He certainly will try to "work" or worry you. Here is a method that has brought me considerable success.

Walk up to the bat and bluff as if you didn't care whether you struck at anything or not; that your main purpose was to have the pitcher throw four balls and let you walk. Give him the impression that you have no respect for his control.

In a situation like this the pitcher will usually center his efforts on getting the ball over. In a desire to show you his control he may pitch nothing but a straight ball, right over the middle, especially if he thinks you are not going to strike at it.

Then, as soon as you see a good one, step forward and take a sock at it.

Nine times out of ten it will be a peach. On the next trip, if the pitcher indicates that he is going to fool you with the first one, simply wait. The idea is to keep the pitcher guessing instead of letting him put you on the anxious seat. It is largely a matter of psychology. You may not out-think the pitcher every time but you will certainly improve your own mind in trying.

As to the opposing infield, always try to keep them guessing as to whether you will swing hard or bunt. If they are uncertain you will often get a hit on an infield grounder or a bunt. Never let them recognize your intentions by the way you stand at the plate. If they are playing deep, try a bunt. Then, if you see them moving in as if for a bunt, why, hit the ball hard and smash it through. To do this, I realize that your eye must be keenly trained. It is not as easy as falling off a log, but you will be surprised at the number of times you succeed. You will also get a great delight of playing a game of wits. In a short time you will be respected as a smart ball player. Once you get that recognition your job becomes easier.

Now, when you step up to swing at a ball, get all the length possible from your shoulders to the tip of your bat. Let the bat out of your hand as far as possible. Your arm should be like a continuation of the bat. In golf, this is called swinging through, and is all-important. There is an important difference, however. In baseball you should chop at the ball. You should take a short, sharp swing and still keep your arms in the position I have described. The long swings may knock a ball out of the lot occasionally, but you get much better results by meeting it squarely with a sharp chop. The only excuse for taking the big swing is to throw the infielders off their guard.

Every boy probably has discovered by this time that there is one pitcher whom he does not seem able to hit. That follows a man right through the big leagues. For a long time I had an awful time learning to hit "Doc" White.

If this trouble has come to you, you must get busy immediately and find out just what is the fault.

There are various remedies. One of the best is to shift your position in the batter's box. Try several positions until you find what you think is the right one. If you do not succeed you may next try different ways of holding your bat. You can increase your accuracy and confidence by "choking" it, that is, moving your hands farther up so as to make the swing shorter. On the other hand, if you have been accustomed to "choking" the bat let your hand slip down toward the end so that you can take a long free swing.

If you will keep trying persistently and with purpose you will eventually find the trouble. Then you can correct it. Above all, don't allow yourself to get upset over it. If you start worrying it is possible that your efforts at making changes will make you worse. Think the matter out carefully, realizing that the fault is yours, and try one theory at a time.

My old friend Hans Wagner, one of the greatest batters that ever lived and a very close student of the art, says that when a batter goes into a slump against some particular pitcher or against all of them he will usually find the fault in his feet. Hans says that the position of the feet and the legs is more important in batting than anything else. This is another way of saying that the stance is everything. Unless a batter feels easy and comfortable he can not keep his mind on the ball.

Shown here in 1911, Honus Wagner of the Pittsburgh Pirates was always considered a friend by Ty Cobb. The only time their teams met on the diamond was in the 1909 World Series, when they each led their respective leagues in batting. Pittsburgh won the contest handily. After much fan anticipation about the Wagner-Cobb match-up, Ty Cobb's performance was well below that of Wagner's. *Courtesy: Library of Congress, Bain Collection*

Ty Cobb in his batting stance in 1910, showing his famous "split grip." Ty used this grip in order to adjust his swing to each pitch thrown, and thus be able to place a hit to any field. In the 1909 World Series against Pittsburgh, Ty discovered that Honus Wagner, who led the National League in batting, shared this unique bat grip. *Courtesy: Library of Congress, Bain Collection*

Chapter 22

"The art of stealing signs"

The cycle of sign stealing in baseball—mind you players never use the word "signals," but always "sign"—was at its height in the days of the great Athletic Club of Philadelphia up to 1912 or 1913. I mention the Athletics because they had developed the art of stealing signs of their opponents to a high degree. No other club has ever approached them for keenness in detecting the catcher's instructions to a pitcher.

In the minds of the public there seems to be an impression that sign stealing is illegal—at any rate, unsportsmanlike. It is not so regarded by ballplayers. If a player is smart enough to solve the opposing system of signals he is given due credit. It is part of the game. I refer, of course, to detecting signals while on the field in actual contest.

There is another form of sign stealing which is reprehensible and should be so regarded. That is where mechanical devices worked from outside sources, such as the use of field glasses, mirrors and so on, by persons stationed in the bleachers or outside the center field fence.

Both of these methods have been used in the big league. People who tell you otherwise are simply not aware of what went on during those days. It should be remembered, however, that signal tipping on the field is not against the rules, while the use of outside devices is against all the laws of baseball and the playing rules. It is obviously unfair.

The most flagrant case of outside signal tipping that was discovered during my early days in the league was at the old American League park in New York on Washington Heights. That affair created quite a disturbance—almost scandal—among ball players at the time. The public, it seems, never knew much about it.

In centerfield there was an extra fence inside the regular boundaries of the park. This was covered with large advertising signs. On one of them was painted a very large derby hat. This hat sign was used to detect the catcher's signs. A hole had been cut in the crown of the black hat. A man stood behind this and leveled a pair of field glasses on the catcher's hands. As soon as he got the sign he would tip the batter off by raising or lowering a board across the hole in the hat.

Battery signals are not as elaborate as some seem to think and are comparatively easy to understand if any one can see the catcher place his hand in his mitt. Nearly all signs are given that way. They have to be simple so as to be observed quickly. For example, a catcher will put one finger in the palm of his mitt for a curve ball; two fingers for a fast ball, and maybe three for a slow one. He may draw his finger through the dust for a pitch-out. These signals are varied by the use of the doubled up fist or something like that. Anyway, they are not difficult to read and understand after a man has watched them for a while from a point of vantage.

This man hid behind the derby hat. Most ballplayers know the identity of that man now, but I won't mention it for fear that I might be mistaken. Anyway, he was not a player on the New York team.

Bill Donovan, one of the smartest pitchers that ever lived, was first to discover that something was wrong. He noticed that the Yankee batters would walk up and hit at what he offered with perfect confidence. He discussed this on the bench and passed it along to the other clubs.

The next time we came to New York, Donovan was determined to satisfy his curiosity. We had watched everything closely without discovering the trick. So, while he was not pitching, Donovan slipped out as if to go to the clubhouse. By sneaking along between the two fences he discovered the signal tipping devices. The man had got wind of his coming and had escaped, but there was the device.

The cleverness of the Athletics in stealing signals and disconcerting their opponents was a result of combined study and thought. It was all done on the field and was legitimate. They took no advantage, because the other club had exactly the same chance of discovering the Philadelphia signals. The difference was that other Clubs never mastered the art so perfectly.

The only opposing player who has a real chance of discovering the pitching signals is a runner on second base. From that point he can look into the catcher's hands just as well as the second baseman and the shortstop. If he is quick of eye he can detect the difference in the signs for a curve ball or a fast one. By comparing notes with the next runner they can soon get onto the system. But the art is in doing it without the opposing club getting wise to it.

The Athletics worked many ways of using this information after they got it. Danny Murphy was extraordinarily clever at it. In fact, he could even solve the signals system from his position in the coacher's box. Naturally the base runner could not tip off the batter very well. But he could inform the coach so that no one would know from whom the batter got the tip.

In these battles of wits we often have changed the signs so as to confuse the Athletics, only to have them catch the new ones in an inning or two. In those days—that cycle of signal tipping—nearly every club had a player who was an expert at catching the signs. The clubs laid great stress on it. There is certainly some advantage in clubs knowing what the pitcher is going to throw or when the hit-and-run play is to be attempted, but I really think the importance of it is exaggerated.

The players used to tell of Al Bridwell, toward the end of the season, being given the signs and failing to profit by it. Bridwell, who had been a Giant, was then on the Boston club. The pennant was already decided and Brid's old teammates wanted to see him hit .300. On the last day Bresnahan not only let him know what was coming, but asked Brid what he would like to hit. Then he would signal for it. With this great advantage Bridwell went to bat five times and didn't get a hit. He always said after that he would rather not know what was coming.

Chapter 23

"A lesson in base running"

In this narrative I am jumping from pillar to post, but in doing so I am letting the fans guide me.

"Why not go ahead with those informative and instructive articles on the science of the game," writes Mr. Victor Gilpin from New York, "and give the college boys and other amateurs a lesson in base running? I know they would appreciate it."

Mr. Gilpin was kind enough to say some complimentary things that I would rather not put in my own memoirs.

I like to talk and to write about base running. To me it is the one great art of the game, the most fascinating. I also regret to say that with the advent of the lively ball many ball players are allowing base running to become a lost science. If that continues baseball will become simply a cut-and-dried affair of hitting the ball and running.

In base running as in batting, the eye should always govern you. Keep your eye on the ball every minute. Make a point of studying the actions and mannerisms of the opposing fielders. Concentration will do this much more rapidly than you may suppose. Take them one at a time and study their habits so as to have a pretty good idea what they will do in certain circumstances. Some men will return the ball quickly whether a play is intended or not; others will fuss around with it to see what the base runner intends to do. It is easy to spot them.

Now, if you observe a fielder who habitually fusses with the ball, you will often be able to take two bases instead of one. The same may be said of the catcher. Study him closely and you will have a pretty good idea when to steal.

By studying the psychology of my opponents I soon caught the knack of taking an extra base. I managed to play them instead of letting them play me, an idea that old George Leidy instilled in me way back in my early days.

Eddie Collins has often told me that the best base-running play I ever pulled was at his expense and because he took it for granted that I would act in a certain way. He has sent me an article he wrote about this for a magazine.

In a game against the Athletics I had hit a two-bagger into deep right center. It was good for two bases, but apparently no more. I had studied the fielder and knew his manner of lobbing the ball up when there was no play, or in making a sudden throw to second when he thought the runner would go too far over the bag.

In this play I ran down to second, going about eight feet over the bag, where I pulled up as if to stop. The idea of three bases seemed out of the question. I stopped as if to walk leisurely back to the bag. Just then the fielder shot the ball to Collins. He swung around as if to touch me. Instead of stopping though, I took a fresh jump and started for third, just as the ball was thrown. Barry yelled to Collins too late. As he swung around to touch me I was shaking the dust off my clothes at third.

Now, the point I make is that any ball player, even with ordinary speed, could do that. There are many faster men than I. My advantage came in having studied the way those two players handled two base hits.

But Collins was too smart to ever let me do it again. He studied me after that and we used to have some great battles of wits.

The main thing in base running is to perfect your judgment of distance and speed. In going from second to third, for example, a player should never be caught. He should have enough lead before he starts. He should know his own speed and that of the ball. If he has the lead he will steal the base successfully. If he hasn't enough lead, he should never start. That sounds simple and it is simple. Don't be afraid of it.

All base stealing depends principally upon the lead a runner takes off the base. You should make a point of getting just as far off the bag as possible, but not so far that there will be any danger of your being caught off. Much practice of this will soon train your mind. The most important point is to always have your body in position where you can dart back to the bag just as easily as you can take the jump toward second. Keep your feet pretty well together, so that you cannot be caught flatfooted—that is, unable to start in either direction quickly.

Many bases are stolen because the infielders are caught napping. A good base-runner will try to keep them nervous and apprehensive every moment. Make a false start as often as you please, the more the better. By being constantly on your toes and active they will be in doubt. At the same time make a point of studying them. Often you can tell by the way a second baseman or shortstop moves instinctively toward the bag which one of them is to cover. You can also tell by the mannerisms of the catcher—some catchers—when he is getting ready to make a throw. In other words, keep them watching you, so that you can study them. You must know accurately, of course, the speed of the ball going to second and also your own speed. By timing the two exactly you will succeed.

A guiding principle of mine is to always keep the other man anxious. Try to get on his nerves instead of letting him get on yours. After hitting a long single it is often easy to take an extra base if you will only watch closely. Remember that a defensive play is harder to make than an offensive one. You may slide about the base and have the baseman drop the ball, or the outfielder's throw may not be accurate. The chances of luck are all with the base runner. So, if the fielder is at all slow in picking up the ball, put on fresh speed and take a chance. That is enough to give you the decision. Above all, in base running never be afraid to take chances. The defense has lots more to lose than you have.

Chapter 24

"The unhappy incident in New York"

I have often heard—have even seen it printed in newspapers—that I was not sensitive to newspaper criticism: that I didn't care what the paper said about me or what impression I gave the fans.

Some unkind critics have gone so far as to offer the opinion that this was due to egotism or swell-headedness on my part. They have charged me with deliberately nagging the spectators into outbursts against me.

I don't believe there was ever a person any more sensitive to harsh criticism than myself, especially if it be unjust criticism. Incidentally, ball players are often very unjustly criticized, and it is the rarest thing in the world that they ever have a chance to explain or correct wrong impressions. Publicly they are at the mercy of the newspapers and the fans. I have found, however, that newspaper men and fans are individually fair minded and always ready to hear the ball player's side of a controversy if he has the opportunity to present it to them. He seldom has, though.

If you will stop to think that the great guiding instinct of any ball player, if he be ambitious at all, is to please the public. It will be better understood how really sensitive he is to public criticism. The only way he knows is through the newspapers. If the ball player does not create a desire among the fans to see him he is a failure.

In my youthful enthusiasm very likely I was carried too far many times and did things I should not have done. Everybody has. Those things are often taken too seriously by the public. Once he gets in the limelight the ball player, you understand, is considered as a mature public character when, as a matter of fact, he is but a boy. He has just reached the age of mental poise and balance when he has to retire from the game.

It was during the season when I first won the batting championship—my third year with Detroit—that I got my big thrills of newspaper publicity. I saved every clipping. Looking them over now I find the articles of praise and just criticism far outweighed the unfair ones. Unfortunately, though, it is a human trait to remember the unkind things after the nice ones are forgotten.

My first big plunge into headlines was over the unhappy incident in New York when I jumped into the grandstand and attacked a fan by the name of Lueker. I was immediately the center of a storm that grew until the American League was upset by a strike of the Detroit players.

Since beginning these memoirs I have been asked frequently to give the facts about that incident. Some of the letters carry a veiled intimation that I would prefer to forget it. Nothing is further from the truth. I will always cherish memories of that affair because it brought home to me the real loyalty of my teammates and of my friends among the spectators. To this day I believe that under the same circumstances I would do the same thing again.

You readers have little idea of the terrible insults and abuse to which ball players have to meekly submit. The few outbreaks are the exceptions that prove the rule. They indicate how much the ball player has had to endure before breaking out of harness.

It is impossible for me to make fully clear the provocation that afternoon in New York because the remarks, even in their mildest form, are unprintable.

This particular fan, always seated back of the visitors' bench, had abused me on previous occasions, but I had pretended not to hear it. This day, for some reason that I do not know, he started on me worse than ever. The foul epithets and other coarse remarks in plain hearing of several women fans were unbearable. I stood it for three or four innings and my submission appeared to make him worse.

Finally, as I came back to the bench he made a remark to me that no self-respecting man could fail to resent under any circumstances. The papers at the time, trying to get the idea to the public without saying the actual language, said that he called me a "coon."

"Hey, you coon, what are you doing on a team with white people!" I quote from one clipping before me.

That, however, gives no idea of the vileness of the remark and the shocked look on the faces of the ladies and the men fans who overheard it. No white man of honor could take it.

"Say, Ty," two or three of the Detroit players said to me, "If you stand for that you are no kind of man. We'll back you up. Go get him."

But I was already on my way. Had I failed to go after that man I could not have looked my teammates in the face.

In a rage I leaped over the boxes, and running toward the man I was ready to swing. Even then he insulted me again. I struck him several times and knocked him out.

The next day I learned from the newspapers that the man was a cripple; that he had lost the fingers from both hands. Of course, I did not know that. I don't know how I could have acted differently if I had known.

Several spectators called to me that I had done right. The rest of the grandstand was in a big hullaballoo.

I was put out of the game by the umpires and went to my hotel still boiling with anger. At any rate, I felt that I had stood up for the rights of the ballplayer, and of the spectators who were not protected from such language.

The next morning the storm broke. Every paper in the country carried headlines about the incident. Then I received a telegram from President Johnson that I was suspended indefinitely—suspended, mind you, without a hearing.

"We'll stick by you," declared the players. "This thing has got to come to a showdown." And they did stick in a most sensational way.

Claude Lueker, the New York fan who heckled Ty Cobb on May 15, 1912, prompting Cobb to enter the stands and attack him. This incident resulted in Ty Cobb's ejection and suspension, and precipitated the first baseball strike. Ty's Detroit teammates felt that he was justified in attacking this abusive fan, and that he had been unjustly suspended by League management without a fair hearing. Lueker made this statement about the incident: "He let out with his fist and caught me on the forehead, over the left eye. You can see the big lump over there now. I was knocked over and then he jumped me. He spiked me in the left leg and kicked me in the side. Then he booted me behind the left ear. I saw that the Detroit players were wading into the crowd with their bats, but I did not see anybody hit. I was down and couldn't see much anyway." This statement indicates the support Cobb had from his Detroit teammates, and implies that other Tiger players may have entered the stands to attack hecklers as well. Several sportswriters reported at the time that Cobb recognized and targeted Lueker in the stands because Lueker had heckled Cobb in numerous previous games. One sportswriter stated that Ty actually knew Lueker from his time in Georgia, but this purported relationship was never described in detail. *Courtesy: Baseball Magazine*

During his 17-year major league career, Christy Mathewson won 373 games and lost 188. His career ERA of 2.13 and 79 career shutouts are among the best all-time for pitchers. Mathewson used a good fastball, outstanding control, and a new pitch he termed the "fadeaway" (later known in baseball as the screwball) to record 2,502 career strikeouts against 844 walks. According to Ty Cobb, Matty seldom, if ever, threw a spitball. Mathewson served with Ty Cobb in the Army's Chemical Warfare Unit during the last months of World War 1.
Courtesy: Library of Congress, Bain Collection

Chapter 25

"A bond of friendship was sealed"

There were times in my first two seasons when I thought harshly of some of my team mates, and they thought harshly of me. That, however, passed when I got into my first real trouble, following the thrashing of that insulting fan in the old American League park in New York. Right then, a bond of friendship was sealed. It has never been broken.

After all, the only real test we have of loyalty is when a man is in trouble. The next morning after that affair, of which the newspapers made a sensation, I was notified by telegraph from President Johnson that I had been indefinitely suspended.

"It's a shame, and we won't stand for it," my team mates declared. "A ballplayer has some rights that must be respected."

"He, at least," said Jim Delehanty, "should be given the same right as a criminal—should have a hearing."

Our next series was in Philadelphia with the Athletics. By the time we reached there the players were highly indignant over the treatment accorded me. They finally held a meeting, and decided to refuse to play until my suspension was lifted. This was not done so much as a personal tribute to me as for the fact that I happened to be the one who resented a string of unbearable insults. The players, as I have said before, told me that day if I did not resent the abuse of this fan I wouldn't be a man: that if I did they would back me up.

I had forgotten that remark, but they didn't. They struck.

Personally I did not want the players to go on strike because I knew that it would lay them open to punishment. I was willing to be the goat. But they refused to listen to me and acted without me.

This telegram was sent to Ban Johnson:

"Feeling Mr. Cobb is being done an injustice by your action in suspending him, we, the undersigned, refuse to play in another game until such action is adjusted to our satisfaction. He was fully justified in his action, as no man could stand such personal abuse from any one. We want him reinstated or there will be no game. If players cannot have protection we must protect ourselves."

This was signed by every player on the club excepting myself and Hughie Jennings, the manager. The so-called strikers were: Sam Crawford, Jim Delehanty, Davy Jones, Oscar Stanage, Oscar Witt, George Moriarty, John Ouslow, Edgar Willett, William Burns, W. Covington, Paddy Bauman, William Louden, George Mullin—all of them, in fact. I remember those names offhand.

You can well imagine my state of mind. I lay awake at night thinking of how loyal the players had been to me and to their rights. At the same time I felt guilty at having put them in this plight, from which there was little chance of escaping without severe punishment.

I thought then—I still think—it was a most unjust thing to suspend without a hearing. I had done what I thought was right; had upheld my honor, and here I was suspended indefinitely and no sign of an immediate hearing. That is one custom in baseball that ought to be abolished. But it hasn't been changed. A ball player is still without adequate protection from insult and if he resents it he is suspended just as I was. In the theatre, if a spectator insults an actor he is ejected immediately. The officials and the police are supposed to do that in baseball now, but they don't always do it.

When President Johnson received the telegram he did not reinstate me. As a result, the players went out to the park,

waited until a short time before the game and returned to the
hotel.

In the meantime, Manager Jennings, placed in an awkward
position, had been given sufficient warning and he got together
a crowd of amateurs and semi-pros. The regular players turned
over their things to them and a game, such as it was, was played
with the Athletics.

In the meantime the whole league was upset by the sensation.
The striking players reaffirmed their determination not to play.
Ban Johnson came to Philadelphia on a fast train and so did Mr.
Navin, owner of the Detroit Club. Meeting after meeting was
held to no avail. Neither side would give in.

The Detroit players were flooded with telegrams offering
them jobs with outlaw leagues. The situation was getting
worse.

After several powwows the league officials agreed to take up
the question of upholding the rights of players. It was decided
that the request for my reinstatement would not be granted, but
that the striking players would be reinstated immediately and
that any fines assessed would be settled in a way not to hurt
them. They never paid them out of their own pocket.

I went to the meeting and asked the players to go back while
waiting disposition of my case. I felt, and so did the other players, that they had won a victory by forcing the leagues to take
steps to respect their personal rights.

The leading influence in this adjustment was the regard the
players had for Mr. Navin. He, after all, would be the main
financial loser.

I had a feeling that my punishment would not be as severe as
had been indicated, and it wasn't. A small fine was imposed on
me and I was back in the game in ten days.

The feature of all the trouble that appeals to me, however,
was the loyalty and friendship of my team mates. My ambition
increased ten-fold. I thrust all my soul into the game and fought
with every ounce to win the pennant. The whole team took on a
feeling of solidarity, and I believe the inspiration of the strike
had much to do with our landing the championship.

Chapter 26

"Create a mental hazard for the opposition"

A common error, and a costly one, in baseball as well as in other professions, is to underestimate the ability of your opponents or competitors. Many a man has failed because he considered the other fellow a sap.

I would suggest to a youngster entering the big league that he bear in mind the fact that at least two hundred players got their jobs on practically the same qualifications. To assume that he can outthink them easily is quite a presumption. Their ways of doing things may be different and their mannerisms in speech may be different, but they are usually equipped with the same mental machinery.

Personally I always had more success in figuring that my opponents had about the same amount of brains that I did, and that under similar circumstances they would follow the same line of thought. Most people like to think that they are different from the average person, but in reality they are not. The statistics of the insurance companies prove that pretty well, I think. Their calculations are based on the average man and they work out with exactness.

Always I have been interested in psychology, and used it to advantage before I knew it to be a particular scientific study. Often it has been said in the sporting columns of the newspapers that I took reckless chances in baseball and got away with them through sheer audacity. In fact, I never did anything of the kind. I rarely took a chance that I had not figured out carefully in advance. I tried to make it appear, however, that I was acting on sudden impulse and relying on luck. I was able to do that through a respect for an opponent's ability rather than through disregard for him.

As I have previously remarked I have been a close student and an admirer of Napoleon. Everything that he did interests me. He it was, I believe, who said in effect: "The secret of success in warfare is to put yourself in the position of your opponent and decide what you would do under the same circumstances. Then do something else. The chances are he will think as you do."

That is not an accurate quotation, but it conveys the idea that impressed me: the one that I found it worth while to follow.

For example, I have often gone to bat with a desire to hit at the first ball, knowing that the pitcher had control. After a moment's thought I would realize that the opposing pitcher, just as wise as myself, would expect me to make a move like that. Consequently he would decline to lay the first one over as he had been doing to other batters.

Instead of hitting I would let the first one go by and take a chance on a later pitch. I recall doing this twice to Ed Walsh. The third time up he had decided that I was playing a waiting game and tried to cross me by putting the first one squarely over. That was exactly the frame of mind that I was trying to get him in, and when he turned loose the fast ball through the middle of the plate, I clipped it for a clean hit. I was able to outguess Rube Waddell that way.

When on first base and contemplating a steal I used to study the mannerisms of the pitcher closely to see when he intended throwing to the plate and to the base. I knew he was feeling me out to see when I intended to start. Two or three times I would take the jump on the second ball pitched, for example, whether I had any hopes of making it or not. I would then put myself in the pitcher's position and figure that "Cobb has worked out a set system of going on the second pitch."

Then when a critical moment arrived in the game and I had a chance, I would start on the first or third pitch—the one he didn't expect. It is surprising how often you can cross up a pitcher that way. The scheme succeeded because of my faith in his intelligence rather than in my considering him a numskull.

The real idea is to give the other fellow credit for brains and then decide your own moves accordingly. If it develops that he really hasn't much intelligence, you are just that much better off.

This trick of making some move repeatedly just to throw an opposing team off its guard is what I always called my "Threat." It is the same idea as an army demonstrating its strength in one direction and then delivering the blow from another quarter.

Batters often make a threat to bunt when they never intend to lay the ball down. Their purpose is to draw the infield in closer and then hit the ball hard. That is a very common move. The smart pitchers get on to it and often cross the batter by signaling the infield to keep back.

That is the time for the batter to be alert. If he sees that they are not falling for his bunt threat he can go right through with it. It is a rather dangerous move, but I have seen batters break up a ball game by bunting on the third strike and taking a chance. Of course, if he fouls the ball he is out; but that is the chance he has to take.

The whole idea is to create a mental hazard for the opposition by continually mixing the players up as to your plans.

Cy Young was notoriously difficult to steal bases on, having a unique ability to hold runners near the base. Over time, Ty Cobb was able to discover a certain "tip-off" in Young's delivery, which told him when Young would make a pitch to the batter, rather than a pick-off attempt at first base. After testing this finding, Ty was able to increase his lead off base, and successfully steal against this future Hall of Fame member. Cy Young pitched for five different major league teams in his 22 year career. He set the record for most career wins (511), as well as most innings pitched (7355), most career games started (815), and most complete games (749). He also won at least 30 games in a season five times, with ten other seasons of 20 or more wins. *Courtesy: Library of Congress, Bain Collection*

Bill Donovan, pitcher with Detroit from 1903 to 1912, questioned how the Philadelphia Athletics hitters could consistently anticipate his pitches. On investigation, he discovered a person with field glasses reading the catcher's signs and signaling them to the batters from behind the outfield fence. Donovan later managed the Yankees from 1915 to 1917, winning 220 of 465 games that he managed. *Courtesy: Library of Congress, Bain Collection*

Chapter 27

"Speed is only a part"

"Is it true," a fan asks me in a letter, "that some slow men are better base runners than fast men? Will you explain this more fully."

Yes, it is true, and for the simple reason that speed is only a part of the equipment necessary to make a successful base runner. As I intimated before most of the bases are stolen off the pitcher and not off the catcher.

A slow man, by studying the pitcher closely, can often take a lead big enough to offset any advantage that some fast men may have in speed. If a player will only concentrate on discovering the various little mannerisms of his opponents—especially the pitchers—he will discover many things to his advantage. Nearly all pitchers make some little muscular move or assume some odd position when intending to throw to the plate or to first base.

One of the most satisfying days of my life was when I finally discovered one of these little faults or "tip offs" in the delivery of old Cy Young. If you older fans will remember, Young watched the bases very closely. It was almost impossible for a runner to take a big lead off first base. Consequently, it was considered very difficult to steal a base on Cy Young. If a runner gets a big enough lead he will steal the base regardless of how swiftly the catcher may throw.

I was determined to steal on Young and in time I succeeded.

For a long time older players were puzzled to know how I managed to do this when crafty old Cy was holding up the other base runners.

One day while watching Young from the bench I noticed the way he held the ball when a runner was on first base. It took me several innings to be sure, but finally I had proved the truth of my discovery to my own satisfaction.

Young had a way of holding the ball with both hands and resting it on his chest just before he made his motion to throw to the plate. If he intended throwing to first base to check a runner he would hold the ball in both hands as usual, but would raise them off his chest and up close to the point of his chin. He thought he was holding the ball the same way in both situations, but a subconscious suggesting, I suppose, caused his hands to make that slight change in position.

Before I decided to act on this discovery I watched until old Cy had worked that way on eight different occasions. The next time I got on first I took the chance. Cy expected me to take a lead and kept the ball close up to his chin, meaning that he would make a snap throw to the bag. I kept close to the bag then, but when he dropped them down to his chest I made a lunge toward second and had a ten foot lead before he threw at all. Having started his motion he couldn't stop and had to throw to the batter. I stole the base without having to slide,

I kept this secret until I had demonstrated it several times. Then I gave it to our other base runners. I don't think Cy Young, marvelous old pitcher that he was, ever did know how I managed to take that lead on him and get away with it. He never did change the position of his hands.

One Spring a new young pitcher came into the league with all kinds of stuff. It was very difficult to do anything with him at the bat. On the bases, though, we could run at will. Studying him closely, we discovered that when he intended making a throw to catch a runner napping off first he would lift his right heel off the ground and give it an odd little twist. He had no idea that he was tipping us off; but the moment that heel would come off the ground we would stick to the bag. If he stood flat-footed we would take the jump for second.

Stealing third is not nearly such a difficult feat as many fans appear to believe. In fact, it ought to be easier. If a base runner has a good eye for distance and perfect knowledge of his speed he ought to be able to steal third nearly every time he starts. To state it another way, if the runner has any doubts about making it he ought not to start. Once he gets sufficient lead, he knows, or should know, that he can get to the bag before the pitcher can throw to the catcher, and the catcher, in turn can throw to third. It is all a matter of accurate judgment. In case of doubts a runner should not start. Once he does start, he should never be thrown out.

To be a successful base runner I think a man must have natural liking for it as a sort of individual sport, a battle of wits between himself and some other fellow. Some of my greatest thrills in baseball came from taking third and home when I was expected to stop at second. In the old days I always delighted in trying to outwit Hal Chase. That, I may say, was no easy job.

One day in a game at New York I was on first when Sam Crawford hit to the infield and was thrown out at first. I had started with his swing and there was no chance of getting me at second. As I reached the bag I decided to challenge Chase on a play. It always gave me a thrill to beat him. He also liked to nab me.

After touching second I ran thirty feet past the bag as if I was going on to third. Suddenly I stopped. Chase stood at first with the ball in his hand trying to decide whether to throw to second or to third. For a full second we stood looking at each other. Then I lunged toward second and as I did Chase's arm drew back for a throw to that bag. Just as he let the ball go, however, I reversed and bounded toward third. It was too late for Chase to change.

When the second baseman got the ball he whirled and threw to third. As I ran I knew he would throw low so that the third baseman would be in position to get me out. He figured, of course, that I would slide. All this flashed through my brains as I stepped off those fifty or sixty feet. The third baseman got the ball a little to one side. Instead of sliding I touched the inside of the bag with my foot and kept right on for home. When the baseman turned to touch me I wasn't there. Before he could straighten out and make a clean throw to the catcher I had slid over the plate and was safe.

The New York papers made quite a story out of that play and it always gave me a thrill.

Chapter 28

"The battle of all times on the diamond"

The greatest game of baseball played—within my memory—
was that between the Detroit Tigers and the Philadelphia
Athletics on September 30, 1907, which went seventeen innings
to a 9-9 tie, being called on account of darkness.

It was the greatest because it contained practically every element in the game that makes for thrills and excitement. It was
doubly thrilling because of its importance in the race for the
pennant. A victory that day might have decided the pennant
either way. There were pitchers knocked out. The score was
tied in the ninth with a home run. There was a near riot on the
field. There was an umpire's decision that stands to this day as
an example of gameness in the face of a hostile crowd that had
overflowed the stands and stood on the field.

But for a double-header having been scheduled that day such
an exhibition of baseball would not have been possible. Even as
it was, the first went into darkness. As I say, nearly every situation in baseball contributed to make this game stand out as the
battle of all times on the diamond.

The pennant race was very close between our Detroit club
and the Athletics. It was generally believed that the double-
header in Philadelphia would practically decide the championship. Dozens of baseball writers left their own cities and went to
Philadelphia to cover this crucial affair. I have heard many

games called CRUCIAL, but this was the real thing. That word describes it without exaggeration.

When we started to play it was estimated that 40,000 people were in Shibe Park. Thousands of fans sat on the grass of the far outfield, a slender rope protecting the playing field. This crowd figured prominently in the thrilling battle. Some have claimed that the Philadelphia crowd cost its own team the victory. That, I doubt.

This now historic game started with Dygert pitching for the Athletics and Bill Donovan for the Tigers. Dygert was knocked out early, and in came that marvelous left-hander, Rube Waddell. To give you an idea of how Waddell could pitch in those days, he started out with such terrific speed as to strike out six of the first nine batters to face him. We went into the seventh inning six runs behind, but kept right on fighting. We gradually forged ahead until in the first half of the ninth we were just two runs behind. In that inning Sam Crawford hit for a single. I'll never forget the next few minutes when I went to bat, facing the speedy Waddell. When I let a fast ball go by, Rube laid another one within reach. I swung hard and, luckily, had timed my swing with exactness. My bat met the ball squarely and drove it over the right-field fence, out into the street, for a home run. That tied the score. Then came the battle that is still talked about wherever old-time ball players meet.

Rube Waddell was taken out to start the tenth, and Eddie Plank, as smart a pitcher as ever lived, succeeded him. All this time Bill Donovan was pitching steadily and gamely.

In the eleventh we took the lead again when I hit into the crowd for two bases, and Rossman scored me with a single. The lead was short lived though. The Athletics came right back and tied us up.

In the twelfth the Athletics had the bases full, but could not score.

The big storm of the day, the almost tragic event that Philadelphia will never forget, came in the fourteenth. Harry Davis, the first man up for the Athletics, smacked a long fly toward the centerfield crowd. Crawford had judged the ball accurately and was under it standing in the edge of the crowd. Just as the ball struck his hands, a big policeman, unduly excited, deliberately bumped into Sam, giving him the shoulder. The ball was jostled out of his hand and fell to the ground.

Umpire Silk O'Loughlin could not see the play from behind the plate. He called to umpire Tommy Connolly, who was stationed at second base.

"The play was interfered with," said Connolly.

"Then the man's out," declared Silk.

There was an immediate roar from the crowd, the likes of which I never expected to hear again.

Monte Cross rushed out from the coaching lines and in the general hullabaloo got into an argument with Bill Donovan, who finally pushed him away. Cross started to swing on Donovan, but Rossman got in front of him. Several spectators rushed on the field trying to swing at Detroit players. The police took both Rossman and Cross away. It took some time, but the crowd was finally driven from the field and play resumed. Killian relieved Rossman at first base.

The great game was resumed, and we went on to the seventeenth inning fighting every inch of the ground, neck and neck. Neither side, after that, was able to gain an advantage. It then grew too dark to see the ball, and the game was called.

Always I have regarded that decision by Silk O'Loughlin and Tommy Connolly as one of the gamest and most just that I ever witnessed. It would have been quite easy for an umpire, lacking courage or dreading unpleasantness, to have let Davis's long fly go as a two-base hit into the crowd. It would have suited the big crowd certainly, and any protest that we might have made would have amounted to nothing. But those umpires knew what was right and decided the play accordingly. It took nerve and determination to do that.

In answer to numerous inquiries that have been sent me asking for my description of the greatest game I ever saw, or expect to see, I offer the above. It is rare that the stage is so perfectly set for a game like that. But for a double-header having been scheduled, it would not have been possible on account of the lack of time.

I want to add also that Bill Donovan gave that day the greatest exhibition of sustained pitching that I have ever seen. He went the entire seventeen innings without faltering, while the Athletics had to use Dygert, Waddell and Plank.

Chapter 29

"Aces of the game"

In considering the suggestions that I give my views on the great players produced in baseball the first name that comes to my mind, somehow, is Ed Walsh, of the Chicago White Sox. Possibly the game has developed greater pitchers than Walsh, but naturally I must confine myself to those whom I have faced.

My whole baseball career has been limited to the American League, except in the world's series and exhibition games that I have played in. And even though my thoughts turn first to Ed Walsh, the chances are that other batters, just as observing as myself, would select some other pitcher, like Walter Johnson, Eddie Plank, Rube Waddell, Bill Donovan, Cy Young, or Jack Chesbro. I would add to those the names of Addie Joss and Doc White.

If we consider the factor of endurance and consecutive years of pitching efficiency, Walter Johnson's name stands out above them all. I am considering, however, the effectiveness of a pitcher during his best years.

Take, for example, the first five years of Walsh's career and the first five of Johnson's and the edge will be with Big Ed, I believe. Johnson lasted a long time after Walsh was through and for that reason had more lasting value to the game, but the mere fact of Walsh having pitched himself out shows the tremendous effort he put into every game he pitched.

In all baseball I don't believe there was ever a pitcher who could go in to save a game in a pinch and do the job so completely as Big Ed Walsh. Why, I have seen him come into the box with the bases full and none out and promptly strike out the next three batters in a row. I never saw a pitcher who could so effectively smother a rally when called from the bullpen.

In considering pitchers, baseball fans, as a rule, neglect to consider the strength of the team behind the pitcher. Walter Johnson never had a championship team behind him until the last two years but he always had a better fielding and hitting club behind him than Walsh did during his years of greatness with the White Sox.

The White Sox at that time, if you will remember, were called the "Hitless Wonders." The team behind Johnson, during those years, was not much better in hitting but it was immeasurably better in fielding. Walsh had behind him one of the poorest fielding teams that I ever saw. His infield was like a sieve and the outfield was very, very weak.

As a consequence, Ed Walsh always had to win his own game. While Johnson had some real help in those days, Walsh had practically none. That is why I always have marveled at his wonderful individual work. He was indeed a great pitcher.

The fact of Walsh having pitched his arm out so early, as I have suggested, is convincing evidence of how hard and how skillfully he worked. He gave everything to his team, and unfortunately for himself did not figure on the future.

I know that Christy Mathewson was a great pitcher but I never was against him in a championship game and, naturally am in no position to discuss his work intelligently.

Eddie Plank was one of the great pitchers of baseball, ranking right long with Walsh and Johnson. He had everything that a pitcher should have and was extremely clever in the way he used it. In addition to his natural stuff, Plank had several different ways of delivering the ball. His cross-fire was one of the most deceptive deliveries that I have ever seen. Often I have wondered why other pitchers did not develop a crossfire like that used by Plank. Believe me, it was deadly.

Besides that, Plank had brains. Very few pitchers were ever so successful in constantly keeping the batter in the hole. I notice by the records that during my years against Plank I managed to hit .340 and I still wonder how I managed to do that well. There is a saying in baseball that a left-hander is no good when he loses his fast ball. That was not true in Plank's case. He was smart enough to keep right on.

Doc White gave me trouble for a long time. He had a drop ball that fooled me continually. It broke very sharply and was apt to fool anybody who stood well up in the box. I made a long study of White, and finally solved the problem of hitting him by standing far back in the batter's box, so as to get hold of the ball after it broke instead of trying to hit it in front of the plate. I discovered that this drop ball would travel two feet over the plate after it dropped. I was able to reach it.

Addie Joss, who is dead now, gave me a lot of trouble. He was a smart pitcher with a lot of stuff. According to the official records, I did not hit as well against Joss as I did against Plank and Walsh. The figures show that my average against Joss was .253.

Another very puzzling pitcher to me and to our whole Detroit club was Carl Wellman, of St. Louis. He also has passed away. Apparently Wellman did not have so much stuff as the other pitchers I have mentioned, but, somehow, he kept us from getting hold of the ball.

No one could discuss great pitchers—aces of the game—without mentioning Bill Donovan. In that famous seventeen inning game against the Philadelphia Athletics in 1907, he gave one of the greatest exhibitions of pitching skill and gameness that I ever saw. It so happened that I was on the team with Donovan during his years of real greatness and I never knew what it was to bat against him. My admiration for him is necessarily limited to the games I saw him pitch against others.

One of the old members of the New York Giants told me years ago that playing behind Matty gave the same sense as sitting behind three aces in a poker game. That very aptly expresses our feelings when Bill Donovan went into the box in an important game. His very presence inspired confidence. In addition to his pitching greatness Donovan was one of the most lovable characters in the world. The veterans swore by him and the young recruits, so many of whom he helped along in their early days, would fight for him. What a man he was!

Chapter 30

"Study them all, but imitate none"

In reply to some rather interesting inquiries from a college player who has just entered professional baseball my advice to him is: Learn all that you can from recognized star players, but do not try to imitate him in every detail.

This, I should imagine, would apply to young men in any other walk of life just as it does to the ambitious ball player.

I don't believe that any man ever acquired fame without a certain amount of originality. It is equally true that few men ever acquired the knowledge that would inspire originality unless they recognized points of superiority in others and studied those points closely. There are none of us so well equipped naturally that we can not learn from others. Many young fellows have made no progress simply because they listened to those— there are many of that type—who regard a successful batter or pitcher as merely "a lucky stiff."

Most every successful move I have seen made in baseball was the result of careful study and correct thinking—not luck or guesswork. To imitate entirely is merely an admission of weakness. It is also an evidence of mental laziness.

When I first came into baseball I was advised to watch such great batters as Lajoie and Crawford, and to imitate them. Fortunately, for me I did not do that. I watched them closely, though. In doing so I gained a lot of knowledge that I could use in my own way.

For example, I noticed that Sam Crawford, a terrific hitter, always hit at a ball in the same way and from the same position. He was what we call a groove hitter. If a pitcher ever let his delivery slip so as to put a ball in Crawford's groove he would kill it. I noticed also that the moment he came to bat the outfield would shift toward right field. Sam was a dead right field hitter. I tried swinging at a ball in the Crawford style and discovered I could hit it all right, but it occurred to me that if Crawford would change the position of his feet at the bat he could hit the ball in another direction with the same swing.

Crawford never shifted, however. Like Lajoie he had acquired a definite stance at the bat, and it is likely that if he changed he would have lost the rhythm of his swing. I was young and had not acquired so definite a position. It occurred to me, and I proved it to my satisfaction, that the feet and legs had as much to do with the direction and force of hits as the arms. By standing with my feet close together I found that I could quickly shift in either direction. This is very difficult to do from a flat-footed stance with the feet wide apart.

It is much the same in golf. You will notice that golfers like Bobby Jones and other long, straight drivers stand with their feet closer together than the others. It helps the pivot. When a batter or golfer stands with his feet wide apart and flat-footed his legs are apt to become rigid and, remember, rigidity is the deadly enemy of all athletic effort. In baseball we call it getting "tightened up." A batter or golfer must have muscular relaxation to get rhythm. Timing is the whole thing.

Anyway, after studying and admiring Crawford, I made up my mind that I could profit by what I had learned from him, but I would adapt to my own style, or rather I would develop a style to suit myself. I quickly saw the advantage of hitting in all the fields rather than in a certain direction all the time. Instead of letting the fielders play me, I could play them.

Another thing I would suggest to the baseball student is that the batter should not always wait for the ball to be directly over the plate. Much of the most effective batting is done off balls that are a little inside or outside. I never had any patience with the batter who would wait so long that he would be called out on a third strike that slipped over the plate, or a close one that the that umpire called a strike.

Wagner was a versatile batter. He was likely to surprise a pitcher anytime by swinging at a ball that was intended for a pitch-out or a waste ball, as it is sometimes called. He generally hit when he made up his mind to hit whether the ball was over the plate or not. In other words, Wagner was never an imitator. He made a close study of all the other batters, just as I did, and then used that knowledge in developing his own style.

For years young batters, coming into the two leagues, tried to imitate the short, choppy swing of Willie Keeler. They forgot, however that Keeler was a very small, frail man and had adapted that style to his own physical characteristics. Keeler used a little bat that would have suited a boy of twelve or thirteen. With this he was able to make those short, lightning like chops. Willie used his feet to great advantage. By shifting to any position, according to the pitch, he could hit into any field. The fielders were never certain as to the direction he would hit and that uncertainty on their part added materially to his great batting record.

If a young batter watched Keeler and then watched Sam Crawford, I don't see how he could be satisfied to imitate either of them. Their form was a standing example of conflict in style. Why not take advantage of the good points of both?

I notice in late years a lot of youngsters trying to imitate Babe Ruth. That is almost impossible. Ruth has the rare faculty of taking a tremendous swing and at the same time being rhythmical. His natural co-ordination of muscle, eye and timing is remarkable. Just notice his feet and legs, though, and you will see where he gets the tremendous force he puts into a swing.

My correspondent asks me to select one great batter for him to imitate. My answer to that is: Study them all, but imitate none.

Chapter 31

"My All-Star All-Time Team"

Pitchers—Christy Mathewson, Amos Rusie, Cy Young, Charlie Nichols, Walter Johnson, Grover Alexander, Theodore Breitenstein, Eddie Plank **Catchers**—Buck Ewing, Ray Schalk	**First Base**—Hal Chase **Second Base**—Rogers Hornsby **Third Base**—Jimmy Collins **Shortstop**—Hans Wagner **Right Field**—Willie Keeler **Center Field**—Tris Speaker **Left Field**—Joe Jackson

M y selection of the all-star all-time team is based on what personal observation I have been able to make and on information gathered by conversation and correspondence with some of the best authorities we have in baseball. I have made minute comparisons of the old-timers that I did not see, with the players that stood out during my twenty-one years of playing the game. In this way I have formed an opinion as to merit, based on the ability of players to deliver the goods over five or more years in actual competition.

This is not so easy to do as the outsider might think. For example, when I broke in, the pitchers were using their fast ball high, with a good curve and change of pace. The spitball had just been introduced effectively by Jack Chesbro, and very soon there was a sprinkling of spitballers in both big leagues. Then

Bill Donovan, Addie Joss and Fred Glade were so successful with their new style that there was a wave of sidearm pitching.

Consequently, the batters must be considered with due regard for the different forms of pitching they had to face.

It is my firm belief that with few exceptions, especially since the spitball came into vogue, that there have been no pitchers with as much ability as those of fifteen or twenty years ago. The system of pitching changed so radically that the delivery became unnatural and was wearing on the arm. This was particularly true during that long siege of trick pitching, which included the emery ball, the knuckle ball and the shine ball.

Another thing to be considered is that almost every pitcher coming into the game fifteen or twenty years ago had to work himself up through the various minor leagues. When he reached the major leagues he was a finished pitcher and a well-developed specialist in the fundamentals like the fast ball, the slow ball and the curve.

It is my prediction that if trick pitching is completely barred for a period of years, there will be a return to the old styles of pitching. Then there will appear pitchers who may rank with those that I have named for the best of all time: Mathewson, Rusie, Young, Nichols, Alexander, Breitenstein, and Plank.

The present-day fan still marvels at the ability and endurance of Mathewson, Johnson, Alexander, and Plank. They starred over a long period. Rusie, Young, Nichols and Breitenstein, a little further back, were of the same calibre, enduring for many years against all clubs and under the hardest of conditions.

I am aware that my judgment on Plank might be questioned, but I stick by it. He was a man of the best habits in his every-day life and was absolutely dependable. His high winning percentage covered a long period.

I will grant that Rube Waddell had phenomenal ability at times, had a wonderful physique, and had lots of stuff on anything that he pitched. To my way of thinking though, Waddell had no place on a team like this. Waddell would not stand up under punishment. I have known him to lose his head and toss away a ball game, or have to be taken out of the box if some batter happened to slash a line drive through the box. The Detroit club had a regular system of getting him out of the box by dragging the ball to the first baseman, forcing Waddell to cover the base, and sliding into him. As a rule, when that happened he was through for the day. He didn't like the gaff.

There is little use in my enumerating the wonderful points of the other pitchers that I have selected. I do want to add one thing, though. I consider Cy Young one of the greatest pitching machines that I ever have seen. Just to give you an idea! He won over 500 games in the major leagues. That is more games than most of the pitchers of the last twenty years have even pitched in. In other words Young won more games than many of the great stars ever pitched.

Christy Mathewson was another of the Young type. Not only did he pitch well at times, but he pitched often. I will devote a little more space to a game that I saw him pitch in a subsequent article.

In my next article I will take up my selection at the catchers of all time and give my reasons for naming them. I will also attempt to make clear my reasons for putting Chase, Hornsby, Collins, Wagner, Speaker and Jackson on the all-star, all-time ball club.

Harry Heilmann began his major league career in 1914 as a teammate of Ty Cobb. When Ty assumed the Detroit Managers position in 1921, he took special interest in Heilmann, working extensively with him to refine his batting style. With this new style, Heilmann improved his batting average by a staggering 85 points in 1921, leading the League with a .394, and edging out Manager Cobb by five points for the American League batting title. His batting average was .378 for the five years he played under Manager Cobb, and he achieved a career high in 1923 of .402. He played 15 years with Detroit, and then two years with the Cincinnati Reds of the National League. He finished with a career batting average of .342 and was elected to the Hall of Fame in 1952. *Courtesy: Library of Congress, Bain Collection*

Guy Harris "Doc" White of the Chicago White Sox, shown here at Hilltop Park in 1912, was the most difficult pitcher for Ty Cobb to learn to hit. After long study, Cobb found he could hit White's sharply dropping curveball by standing at the back of the batter's box, and hitting the ball after it had dropped and crossed the plate. Doc White pitched for the Phillies in 1901 – 1902, and then for Chicago for 11 years until 1913. He won a career high 27 of 46 games pitched in 1907, and finished with a career ERA of 2.39.
Courtesy: Library of Congress, Bain Collection

Chapter 32

"All-Star All-Time Team—Catchers and Fielders"

In my selection for the All-Star All-Time baseball club I gave my reasons for naming Mathewson, Rusie, Young, Nichols, Johnson, Alexander, Breitenstein and Plank as the greatest pitchers of the game.

For catchers I chose Buck Ewing and Ray Schalk. My other choices were: First base, Chase; second base, Hornsby; shortstop, Wagner; third base, Jimmy Collins; right field, Keeler; center field, Speaker; and left field, Jackson.

In addition to my own observation and experience, I have had to depend on conversations and correspondence with many of the recognized experts who can go back for thirty years or more.

All of the old-timers—to a man—tell me that Ewing was a whale of an all-round ballplayer in addition to being a great catcher. He was a great thrower, fine hitter and base runner. It is rare for one player to have all those qualifications.

Of the catchers that I have seen Ray Schalk stands pre-eminent. I have selected him because I don't see how his work could have been improved upon. Schalk has caught for fourteen years and got everything out of his pitchers that was possible to get. He has handled every kind of delivery and has made his pitchers win.

Bresnahan was a great catcher and he had the heart of a great ballplayer, but Bowerman also did a great deal of the catching for the Giants in their day of greatness. If Bresnahan had been as great as Schalk in every particular, I doubt if Bowerman would have had a chance to do such a big share of the work. Johnny Kling, also, was a great catcher, and I would rank him next to Bresnahan after the first two names.

I don't think there is any question about Hal Chase being the greatest-of-all first basemen. He was little short of a genius in throwing, fielding, running and hitting. I rank George Sisler next to Chase on account of his all-round work.

Capt. Anson was a great hitter over a long period of years but he was not a good fielder. Fred Tenney developed first base play to a great extent. It was his marvelous left-handed playing that made baseball people see the advantage of a first baseman being left-handed. Tenney was a real pioneer in the science of the game.

The hardest decision I have had to make is my selection of an All-Star second baseman. I have studied Hornsby and Eddie Collins from every possible angle. Collins stands out as a tough man to pitch to, and he is a great help to his teammates, but on an all-star team these qualities might not be of the same force as they have been on the clubs that he has played on. Every man being an artist in his position, the coaching might not be needed.

So, I give the call at second base to Hornsby for his terrific hitting with his wonderful extra base record. His bomb-proof style at bat cannot be dented. I think Hornsby absolutely the best hitter I have ever seen. In comparison with Lajoie, Hornsby has never had a bad year since he got going. Lajoie had a couple of bad years. Hornsby is a high-class fielder, has a real good arm and can get around the bases. He is going down in history as the greatest of all second basemen, without a doubt.

Now, at shortstop, Hans Wagner is the man. He was a great hitter, fielder and base-runner. Wallace might have been his equal at fielding and even better at going to his right; but one who has ever seen Wagner play cannot forget his destructive force at bat, his base running and his unique work at short. With his enormous hands he literally gobbled up everything that came his way. Herman Long was another great shortstop, as were Bill Dahlen and Hugh Jennings.

For third base I have named Jimmy Collins and have stopped right there. I can see no use in mentioning anybody else.

Though I have selected Keeler, Speaker and Jackson for my outfield, I find myself wanting to place Fred Clarke in left field on account of the way he played the game. He was a slashing hitter, daring base-runner and very aggressive. I liked his style of play.

Clarence Beaumont was also a great outfielder, and so were Jimmy Sheckard, George Burns, Delehanty, Ruth and Heilmann. Burkett, Hamilton and Lange also deserve mention.

Chapter 33

"The best ball club I ever saw"

Before completing my selection of the All-American League and the All-National League teams as well as naming what I regard the best ball club I ever saw in action, let me digress a moment on the trend of baseball. To me it is always a most interesting study—this development of a boyhood amusement into an exact science.

In baseball we have had two great periods of hitting, and strange to say, they were each of five years duration—1893 to 1898 and from 1920 to 1925. The lowest ebb of hitting was from 1912 to 1916. The spitball and other freak pitching were then at their height and the connection between the pitching and the low hitting is quite apparent.

Yet it is also interesting to note that the last great base running cycle started in 1908 and 1909 and ended about 1917. The man who studies the game can draw some valuable deductions from this.

I am frank to say that from 1920 to 1925, inclusive, the standard of baseball was lowered considerably. I lay this to the introduction of the lively ball. One standing proof of the perpetration of this crime in 1925 was the downfall of the Athletics. Just before the ball was changed again they were slashing their way through, driving all pitchers to grief. Suddenly their hits failed to carry up against the fences and then we all discovered what type of ball club they really had.

I mention these things, to make clear my process of reasoning in selecting the star players of both leagues. We have, for example, some nice looking ball players in the American League who show high averages in the last two or three years, but they have not been playing baseball as real stars should.

As a result of the lively ball and the chance for making long drives the fine points of the game in both leagues have been shunted into the background. The ringing base hit and self-defense fielding have been the vogue since the lively ball was introduced.

With great care I have gone over the records of some of the great ball clubs within my memory. As they narrow down to a few like the Athletics of 1911, the Cubs of 1908, the Giants of 1905 and the Tigers at 1909, it makes me smile to think what would have happened if the lively ball had been in use then.

Let me say right here that the best ball club I ever saw in action was the Athletics who played in the world's series against the Cubs and the Giants in those years running from 1910 to 1912. The dates are not well fixed in my mind but I mean the club composed of Plank, Bender, Coombs and others as pitchers, McInnis, Collins, Barry, Baker as infielders.

That was the outstanding ball club to my way of thinking. It not only showed superiority over competition in its own league but won all its world's series clashes with the exception of the one with the Boston Nationals when the Athletics lost four straight.

As a matter of fact, the Athletics lost that series with the Braves on account of overconfidence, staleness, and being off their stride. To illustrate, I know that they did not even "scout" the Boston club. By that I mean, they did not take the trouble to study the Boston batters, the pitchers and so on.

In the American League at that time they told a story of Chief Bender having been sent to New York to watch the Braves. So little did he consider the use of scouting an easy club like Boston that he went out and played golf.

Bender having been sent to New York to watch the Braves,

Deal was a low ball hitter and Gowdy was a high ball hitter.°°°°°
The Athletics did not notice this change in position. In the first
game with runners on the bases, Gowdy came up early. Bender,
thinking of Deal, pitched Hank a high ball and he socked it. On
the bench several of the Athletics players asked Bender why he
had pitched a high one.

"Well," explained Bender, "Deal is ordinarily a low ball hitter,
so I pitched him a high one."

The Chief, in his supreme confidence had got the batting
order confused.

In the series the Athletics were so absolutely sure that many
such incidents occurred. They could be excused for their confidence at that. Among baseball people the Braves were not
regarded so strong as two or three other clubs in the National
League—clubs that the Athletics had already beaten.

It was the carefree way in which the Athletics took this series
that caused Connie Mack to break up the team. The team
really was too good, and what is worse the players knew that.
They won so regularly that it got monotonous and the public lost
interest.

There was never another ball club so clever as the Athletic
crowd in getting the signals of their opponents. They could pull
any play known to baseball and, after trying all the old ones, they
developed a few new ones of their own. In fact, that club had
everything. They had real sluggers, real base runners and real
bunters.

Now if you will bear in mind that the great Athletic team of
that time was made up of prolific run-scorers and powerful hitters when the ball was not lively you can easily imagine what
they would have done with the lively ball. And another thing,
the Athletics made their great record while we were having a

°°°°° EDITOR'S NOTE: The first part of this sentence also appears in the preceding paragraph, a strong indication that there was a typesetting error in the
original Chapter 33. Apparently Deal and Gowdy had exchanged places in
the batting order, thereby confusing Chief Bender. This entire paragraph
is reprinted here verbatim.

long spell of trick pitching. So, with everything against them, as compared with present day teams, they were still the greatest.

I haven't room here to discuss the other great teams that rivaled the Athletics for all-time greatness—such as the Giants and the Tigers—and will have to take them up in my next article.

Chapter 34

"The next best ball club"

In having named the Athletics around the 1910–1912 period as the greatest of all ball clubs within my time, I probably paved the way for considerable criticism of my judgment and stirred up an old argument again. But, having gone that far, I am now about to add fuel to the fire by declaring the White Sox of 1919 to be the next best ball club I ever saw.

I am not jumping at this conclusion. It is the result of much deliberation and careful analysis. That great White Sox club lost much of the historic prestige that would have been its due by the big scandal. So much has been said of the confessed crookedness of several of the players that the public has lost sight of the White Sox of that year as a great ball club.

For sheer ability just think of the pitchers of that 1919 Chicago club: Cicotte, Faber, Williams, Kerr! Where would you find such a quartet today? Then think of Collins and Weaver and Jackson and Felsch and one of the greatest catchers that ever lived—Schalk. Then of the whole outfit managed by the incomparable Kid Gleason. My, that was a club!

Some people will argue that the Chicago Cubs were a greater machine, but I do not think so. Why, when the Cubs were at their best they lost the world's series to the White Sox of 1904 and also to the Athletics in 1910. The Sox of 1906 were not nearly so strong as that team of 1919. Remember another thing—the competition in the National League was not so keen when the Cubs were making their great records. The main opposition was the Giants, a team I will discuss a little later.

I am not so familiar with the old Pittsburgh team of 1913, but I understand it was a powerful organization. From what I have been told, the Pirate team of that time did not rank with the White Sox of 1919 or the Athletics of 1911.

In a previous article I have pointed out why I thought the Athletics of 1911 the greatest baseball machine that I ever saw. They stand head and shoulders over all of them. The White Sox is my second choice.

It is difficult for any one outside of the baseball ranks to fully appreciate what it means to have four dependable pitchers like Cicotte, Faber, Williams and Kerr. A manager could manipulate a club like that in most any way he desired.

The coming of Eddie Collins to Chicago and the presence of Jackson on the club made the White Sox almost as wonderful as the Athletics which Collins had left. There have been mighty few infielders superior to Buck Weaver.

Schalk I have picked as my catcher for the All Star Team of All Time. I couldn't go much farther than that. To sum it up Kid Gleason had a combination that was pretty nearly perfect.

Of course, there have been many great ball clubs, such as the old Baltimore Orioles and the famous Pittsburgh club of twenty-five years ago, but, unfortunately, I did not see them so as to give a personal opinion. I know they must have been great. Ball players do not keep on talking from year to year about a certain ball club unless it had a lot of stuff. You may be sure of that.

We had a pretty good ball club ourselves at Detroit. We won the pennant three times, and, while we did not win a world's series, it was still a great ball club. When a club wins a pennant even once you can be assured that it has ability. They don't do that by accident or luck. But I have purposely restrained from discussing my own club for fear of appearing partisan.

The Pittsburgh club that won the series from the Senators last Fall looked like a good club to me, but it cannot be brought into comparison with that great White Sox team and the famed Athletics.

I am not taking the Pirates of 1925 into consideration. They have had but one year of success. Time will prove their real worth. The Pittsburgh club as I saw it last Fall seemed to lack something in the catching department. It was also a little weak at second and was especially weak at first with Grantham playing. If he has real ability, he didn't get into his stride enough to show it. In other words, the whole Pittsburgh club seems to lack finish. The pitching staff gave no indication of having the cleverness and the stuff that is needed for a great all around team.

You will notice that I have not included any of McGraw's several teams. I never saw his 1905 club, when Mathewson and McGinnity were in top form. In fact, the only Giant teams I have seen have been those since 1900.

My failure to discuss these clubs with the really great ones of all times is really intended as a compliment to McGraw. On account of his wonderful knowledge of the game, he has got wonderful results with teams that were really inferior to those that he was defeating. It would be interesting to see just how far McGraw could go with a ball club so naturally well equipped as the great ones I have mentioned. You can well imagine what history he would make.

Whether he had a good ball club or one with just ordinary ability, McGraw has kept the Giants high up in the fight year after year. Even though he gave the Athletics a great battle in 1911, McGraw's club was not so strong individually.

The more I look back over the last twenty-one years on the diamond the more plainly it seems to me that the two best ball clubs were the Athletics of 1911 and the White Sox of 1919.

Chapter 35

"My All-American League Team"

Pitchers—Walter Johnson, Cy Young, Bill Dinean, Bill Donovan, Ed Walsh, Chief Bender and Eddie Plank **Catchers**—Ray Schalk and "Nig" Clarke **First Base**—Hal Chase	**Second Base**—Eddie Collins **Third Base**—Jimmy Collins **Shortstop**—Bobby Wallace **Right Field**—Willie Keeler **Center Field**—Tris Speaker **Left Field**—Joe Jackson

Picking this All-American League team, I am selecting players on the same basis that I have used in selecting my other all-star clubs:

First—Ability to hit, field, throw and think.

Second—Ability to play ball under world's series conditions, in other words, with the pressure on; ability as a money player.

Third—They must have a record of five years or more.

Fourth—Absolute reliability as to habits—a man who can thrive under tough assignments and wants to be in the game despite injuries; pitchers who will work out of turn, and so on.

I am selecting seven pitchers because that seems to be the fashion in present day pitching staffs. We have there six crack right-handers, just as effective against left-handed hitters as right-handers. I have selected Plank as my southpaw, because he was just as effective against right-handers as left-handers.

Already I have selected Ray Schalk for my All-Star All-Time catcher, and now I am putting "Nig" Clarke with him. Clarke is still catching after twenty-five or twenty-six years in the game. He was very fast on the bases. A true test of a great catcher is his ability to handle a low ball. Both Clarke and Schalk were unsurpassed in this. Clarke could always hit. He tied for the lead of the American League in 1906. Criger and Sullivan also were great catchers.

For first base Chase is the only possible selection. He was in a class by himself. There will never be another like him, in my opinion.

I have selected Eddie Collins over Lajoie, because he can cover more ground. Coming in on a slow hit ball he outclasses Lajoie, and as to going back for pop flies there is no comparison. Collins is a real base runner and Lajoie wasn't. Collins is more of a student, is always coaching every play. For eighteen years Collins has a batting average of .332, which will compare favorably to that of Lajoie. Another angle in which Collins showed superiority was in tagging base runners.

For shortstop I name Wallace because he was one of the greatest fielders that ever lived. He was the best in the world in going to his right and making a throw from back to third. Turner was a wonderful shortstop until his arm went back on him. Chapman, but for his untimely death, might have been the greatest star in American League history. Everett Scott was a great fielding shortstop and a real money player.

Jimmy Collins stands head and shoulders over them all at third base. He was most effective, most graceful—a man without a weakness. He made every play, no matter how difficult, look easy. Bradley ranks next to Collins, in my opinion, and then comes Buck Weaver.

In picking Keeler for right field, I have selected one of the greatest lead-off men that ever lived. He was an artist at the bat. Every one knows about his great place hitting. Ruth and Heilmann are great hitters, but on an all-star team we must have better fielding.

In centre field I name Tris Speaker and quit right there. Nobody else compares to him.

In left field I place Joe Jackson. He was a slugger, a good sure fielder and could cover all the ground necessary. He also had a great throwing arm. Duffy Lewis was a great defensive ball player and a wonderful hitter in world's series, but he would let his spirit drop sometimes during the season.

In reviewing this team I can't find a weakness. Every man endured for a long time. There is lots of base running in this club; they could work a pitcher; they could bunt and had lots of hitting power, no bad arms; all real fielders, and wise.

Chapter 36

"My All-National League Team"

Pitchers—Cy Young, John Clarkson, Christy Mathewson, Amos Rusie, Grover Alexander, Charlie Nichols, Mordecai Brown, and Theodore Breitenstein **Catchers**—Buck Ewing and Roger Bresnahan **First Base**—Fred Tenney	**Second Base**—Rogers Hornsby **Third Base**—Jimmy Collins **Shortstop**—Hans Wagner **Right Field**—Willie Keeler **Center Field**—Bill Lange or Hugh Duffy **Left Field**—Fred Clarke

In selecting this team I take into consideration the same conditions as in the others: extent of service, reliability, habits and thinking.

For example, in naming the pitchers I have selected only those who have proved their worth over a long period of years. For this reason I have not included Dazzy Vance, undoubtedly a marvelous pitcher. His best season was when he won 27 games, I believe, but so far he has had but two or three years of good work. There was a bad spot in the record of Babe Adams when he was sent to the minors after having done wonderful work in the series of 1909 which eliminates him. Five or six years after that he left the big league but came back and has been very dependable ever since.

Mathewson was probably the best balanced pitcher that ever lived. He had a wonderful assortment with perfect control and was a great baseball student. He stands out.

Alexander has won his thirty games or more for three years. He should be listed well up among the great pitchers. Mordecai Brown was not only a finished pitcher but he was one of the greatest fielding pitchers that ever lived.

Naturally I have no personal knowledge of Clarkson, Nichols, Breitenstein and Rusie, but I know from their records and from what old-timers have told me that they were great. It would be unfair to leave any one of the men I have mentioned off an all-National League pitching staff.

There is no question in my mind about selecting Ewing as first catcher. He was a great catcher and a great ballplayer from every angle. He was a deep student of the game; one of the pioneers of its scientific development.

Roger Bresnahan is my second selection because of his aggressiveness and natural baseball instinct. Bresnahan was a wonderful receiver, very aggressive and one of the few catchers who ever have led off in the batting order. He threw himself into the game with every ounce of strength. In the series of 1905 he established himself as an absolutely top notcher. He was the inventor of the shinguard and also improved the chest protector.

In placing Fred Tenney at first-base I also had Frank Chance in mind and had to split hairs over this decision. As a fielder Tenney was in a class by himself, but Chance, though not so brilliant as a fielder, was a great teamwork man. He was very deliberate in fielding and very smooth. He also was a good hitter and a great base-runner.

Other great first basemen were Jack Doyle, Jake Daubert and George Kelly of the present Giants. I must also mention Pop Anson on account of his marvelous hitting, but his fielding did not compare favorably with the others.

Hornsby belongs at second base. His terrific hitting really overshadows his fielding—so much so that fans are apt to forget that his fielding will average up with the other great men in that position. He has a fine arm and can go into the outfield for

Texas Leaguers. To my mind it is impossible to keep Hornsby off that team—or any other team.

For shortstop Wagner stands alone. Old Honus had everything. He could smash 'em, was a great base runner and nothing got away from him at short. Wagner was probably the greatest all around ballplayer in any position in the history of the game.

Herman Long was a truly great shortstop. His fielding was sensational and he could hit. Of the present day shortstops I must make mention of Dave Bancroft. Winning teams are built around shortstops and Bancroft's work proves it. They have had pennant winners wherever he went—Philadelphia and New York. He is likely to build up a winner in Boston.

Jimmy Collins played in the National League at third base before he came to the American. For that reason I have named him as all all-star on both teams. He absolutely stood alone.

I don't think it necessary to explain why I picked Keeler for right field.

In the left field I have placed Fred Clarke. He had everything in the world and was one of the great stars of the game. Clarke was as fearless as a lion, was a slashing hitter, a veritable demon on the bases. He was a real sparkplug.

My selection for center field was the most difficult. These players were very evenly matched: Lange, Duffy, Burkett and Hamilton. I have put Lange first because his name came to me first. He could do everything—hit, run, throw. I understand though, that he was not a finished slider. The records will show you the greatness of the others I have mentioned. I am not sure just whether I am right in putting Lange's name ahead of Duffy and Hamilton. I think I will leave it right there. This thing at selecting an all star team is a serious undertaking. I hope I have not done anyone an injustice.

THE END.

Appendix

A photocopy of two of the original chapters as published in the *New York Evening Journal*.

TY COBB'S OWN STORY

HUFFMAN F

Baseball's Greatest Star Joins Evening Journal Staff of Experts

TY COBB'S MEMOIRS

CHAPTER 1.

EXCEPT for the detailed work of assembling the facts and getting them down on paper, I should not be particularly at ease in preparing these memoirs of twenty years in baseball. I honestly believe that I can remember everything I ever did in my life. To recall facts and incidents comes easy.

The thing that has dawned upon me, however, is how much more important in life it is for a man to remember what he has thought, rather than what he has done. In the average man in any walk of life could start up the ideas that have come to him, few of which are ever carried out, he would be ten times more interested. If he could watch out a system by which he could have three ideas of thoughts tucked away, ready to be drawn on when needed, most every problem, new or old, would be simplified. But when good ideas and good resolutions are not executed they are usually forgotten. We remember the thing that we did. I suppose that is why the words of great philosophers have lived right down through the ages. Those old fellows kept track of what they thought, rather than what they did. A ball player's good legs may give out, but his good thoughts give strength.

Though a ball player must depend on nerve to give him an unusual muscular mechanism, the more valuable asset that he can possibly have is memory. He can develop that himself. Unless he does he will be simply a mechanical ball player, passing eight out of the picture along with his legs and throwing arm.

He Was a "Second Guesser," Too

The idea expressed itself upon me during the last world's series between the Pirates and the Senators. Upon the start it was plain to experienced baseball men that the Pirates had a natural superiority in speed and punch. The only question was if they could get themselves in the right frame of mind to see it.

The Senators, more experienced in baseball and in life, started right in using their heads to deadly advantage. Their knowledge and memory completely blocked the natural superior mechanics of the Pirates.

Next to me sat John McGraw, Honus Wagner and Babe Ruth. We were all there to analyze the games and were determined to do it seriously. Nine times out of ten our ideas expressed in advance of the important plays agreed.

I had known of the marvelous memory of McGraw and of Wagner and I soon found that Babe Ruth was much more of a student and serious thinker of the game than the baseball public generally believes. We were all four in the position of what we know as "second guessers." That is, we could calmly await the development of a play and then decide what should have been done. That is a cinch. We enjoyed it immensely. In other great games we had been on the bench, having to decide on the play before it was made. If our first guess was right we won. The second guesser, you see, can't always be right. He doesn't have to make up his mind until the play is over. Second guessers are far less of a ball player's life, and I guess that books was in my line of endeavor.

They Were Serious Writers

It's much easier for the man who doesn't have to want to say what the President of the United States SHOULD HAVE DONE. If he had to tell the President what action he SHOULD take, he would probably be more generous, more thoughtful, anyway. First guessers are the men who make names for themselves.

Having had experience on the players' bench, we older baseball men now sitting in the grandstand tried to be fair and just. I was impressed by the seriousness with which all of us took our jobs. So keep were we with our notes and serious decisions that we didn't even have time for light talk and joshing. I had

Cobb Points Out Many Ways Baseball Playing Is Help to Young Man

TY COBB'S MEMOIRS

CHAPTER 2.

NOW, as I look back over my twenty years in baseball, the thought has frequently occurred to me: "What have I gained by it? What has it taught me? What have I accomplished? Was it worth the effort?"

In fact, these questions were among the first asked me when I began the preparation of these memoirs. I can see no particular modesty in undervaluing or evading facts that are pretty well known to most every baseball fan in the country. I have won the batting championship on several occasions, and I have acquired my share of fame and money as a professional ballplayer. That, however, would be no answer to the questions that I have asked myself. Certainly, I have accomplished more than that. If baseball success had taught me or gained me no more than that, it surely would not have been worth while.

I could retire from active work right now and be financially independent. I can educate my children in a way that is denied many men to other walks of life. That is a big thing to me. But for baseball the chances are I wouldn't be in the position to do it. The broadening influence of sound education I regard as one of the greatest things in life. Baseball offers that to young men.

The opportunities afforded by travel, observation and contact with men from various sections of the country have broadened my viewpoint on life and have made me more generous toward the ideas and thoughts of others. That I consider one of the greatest benefits of baseball as a profession. One of the first things that impresses a young ballplayer when he comes into the big leagues either and lives at the first-class hotels is the manners and deportment of the other guests. If he has been denied the chance for education and culture he immediately feels the lack of it and desires it. From that moment on he wants to learn and to understand. Being himself quick with and trained as a man of refinement he makes a resolution to live up to that ruling.

Players Learn Finer Things

I have talked to many ballplayers and they agree that their first insight into the broader world and the realization of what education meant is one of the biggest things to be got out of the game. Numbers of them have been so impressed with this as to save up their baseball money and take college courses during the off months. Of course, there are some who do not care and who never improve mentally, but they are exceptional.

There was a time—twenty years ago—that ballplayers would not like ball clubs as guests. Now the most refined hotels in the country seek the baseball patronage. That is certainly an indication of progress.

My days on the diamond have been rather stormy, due to my high-strung nature and rather fiery temper. Later on I will relate some of these rather sensational incidents and will present my side of them, but not in this chapter.

Through these sensational clashes my twenty years in baseball have taught me the necessity of self restraint. In my younger days I have often tried. At least I know that, even in any walk of life most learn self-restraint to be successful and to be comfortable in his mind. It requires no effort to get in a fight on the baseball diamond, but it often requires a big struggle and a getting of touch to keep out of one. Baseball has taught me that. I suppose the same thing applies to other professions, but in baseball there is much more opportunity for flying off the handle and engaging in physical combat. The lesson is more severe. When men have to face each other they soon learn to respect each other's ideas and to become more minded. They learn forgiveness and manliness. That I think pretty well worth while.

Learning Self Restraint.

Index